The western end of Swindon AE Shop again, where every locomotive leaving the works found itself (see elsewhere in this volume – CENTAUR on page 13 for instance) periodically. D830 MAJESTIC on 5 August 1965 is duly undergoing attention after work in the shop behind – this was the loco fitted with twin Paxman 12YJXL engines in place of the Maybach engines, in an attempt by Paxmans to enter the home market. It must have been the practice to 'fuel up' locos here; the large diameter pipe was armoured with a hand-wheel pattern end connection for connecting it to the loco tank fitting. The latter had a self-sealing valve which was pushed open by rotating the hand-wheel. Inside the tank was a float valve which automatically stopped the flow when the tank was nearly full. Occasionally these float valves stuck open, allowing the tank to overflow, not only wasting fuel but also causing contamination problems. An improved type of piston seal was introduced to try and overcome the problem but failures continued for some time after the improved seals had been introduced and the defective valves were found to be still fitted with the old type seals. A visit to the Main Stores confirmed that the improved type of seal was in stock and was being supplied to the section that overhauled the valves. In the Shop carrying out the valve overhaul a conversation ensued with the Fitter engaged on the work: was he getting the new seals from the Stores? 'Oh yes' he replied 'but I've got all these to use up first" pulling open a drawer to reveal it to be full of the old type seal, 'it seems a pity to waste them.' Another problem solved!

DIESEL DAWN
2. THE SWINDON WARSHIPS D800-D832, D866-D870
Gavin Glenister and John Jennison

Acknowledgements:
Thanks to Brian Penney, Nick Deacon, Mike King, Mike Romans, Allan C. Baker, Peter Harris, Chris Mills, Peter Kerslake, Robert Carroll, for extreme patience...

Progenitor. Deutsche Bundesbahn V200 035 at Köln station on 18 August 1958, in glorious juxtaposition with an ancient Teutonic water column. The Warships ancestry is clear, but so is the great difference in size – compare the position of the cab door for instance. Inside that towering body shell a variety of engine/transmission combinations could be accommodated; the DB purchased engines from MAN, Daimler-Benz and Maybach and transmissions from Voith and Mekydro and they could be found in any combination in a given loco. Even though their weight, design, details varied greatly the DB ordered that all the mountings, connections, intakes and so on should be identical. This flexibility and utility was lost in Britain and although the Swindon and NBL Warships were initially designed to accept both Maybach and MAN engines and Mekydro and Voith transmissions, in practice there was no variation from the Swindon Maybach/ Mekydro and the NBL MAN/Voith arrangements.

Diesel Dawn

2. THE SWINDON WARSHIPS
D800-D832, D866-D870
The Future is Hydraulic

None of the many 'Diesel Dawns' of our times has been investigated, evaluated, celebrated, excoriated, praised and derided, more comprehensively in (often) more partisan ways, than that of the Western Region diesel hydraulics. The story of the Warships is a long and complex one which has been explored in any number of excellent publications. It is the intention here to summarise matters while offering at the same time the occasional original insight. One can personally vouchsafe the startling first impression these locomotives made on a young enthusiast in 1959. Sparkling clean, they were a world away from the conservative box-like outlines of our home-grown Brush Type 2s. They were glamorous even, with that curious sloping front and subtle curves, unhindered by design clutter. And the names! It was the big red plates with the stirring serif names that really capped it all; AVENGER for instance, with WARSHIP CLASS added in case you didn't get the point. By the early 1950s the prototype diesel electric main line

locomotives developed from 1947 (10000, 10001, 10800, 10201, 10202 with 10203 still to come) had almost been forgotten it seems, 'left to chug in splendid isolation' as Stewart Joy puts it (*The Train That ran Away*, Ian Allan, 1973). Leaving aside the reasoning at the time, instead BR Works were busily embarked on what would amount to twelve classes of steam locomotives destined to be more or less immediately obsolescent. Only in January 1952 (shortly after BR had at last ceased building *pre-Nationalisation designs* of steam locomotive) did British Transport Commission/Railway Executive recommendations emerge that 'large scale experiments' should be conducted into diesel and electric traction. By this time the vast US railroads had very much gone over to diesel electrics and the French were forging ahead, building on a high powered diesel design that had been worked out even before the War. Not to mention the Germans...

Fast forward three years for Britain to get even the prospect of comprehensive

modernisation in *The Plan for Re-Organisation and Modernisation of British Railways* of 1955. It was belatedly recognised that diesel traction had significant advantages and 'The Plan' duly announced a shift to diesels. Very quickly this 'Modernisation Plan' became a 'Modernisation Plan in a Hurry' which was something rather different. Sober talk of careful evaluation of small numbers of selected prototypes soon went overboard and a wholesale rush to get enough diesel locos as quickly as possible ensued – of which more below...

Already six years of main line diesel development (those forgotten prototypes 'chugging away' as mentioned above) had been lost. The five main line diesels had been working steam diagrams which often included steam-type lengthy layovers between duties and that was when they were not to be found in works or awaiting parts. Of 10800, the 'secondary duties' loco, the less said the better...

Continued page 10.

A well-known view of D800 under construction, 15 September 1957, complete with chalked DB V200-style speed whisker! Construction of the first three, the actual 'Pilot Scheme' examples, was protracted because (as has been pointed out in various published works) D800 was practically hand built, with each jig fashioned alongside as the loco took shape. *The Railway Observer* noted the new diesels under construction amid various 9F 2-10-0s on 3 November 1957: ...*new construction included Maybach diesels D800 with engine alongside and D801/2 bodies complete*... German technicians and engineers were frequently present and at least one married a local girl and stayed in England.

The Warship body structure has been described as 'radical' which it certainly was – under construction at Swindon is what is assumed to be D813.

This would be D818 according to that buffer. In a remarkable procedure the outer skin was pieced together by welding until each side, cab door to cab door was complete; it was then mated up to the framework before being welded on. After this was complete the openings for the windows and so on were cut out. All slackness and play in these side sheets was removed through thousands of spot welds an inch or so apart. The dynastarter for this end is visible in the nose.

Left. D816 ECLIPSE nearing completion in the background at Swindon in early 1960; emblem, nameplate yet to appear. The road occupied by D816 and the ones adjacent to it led outside off to the right, to sidings where we also see D808 and D804 in accompanying photographs and in several others too, in these volumes. To the right of the loco would be the end doors which can be seen in the other views. D816 is apparently having adjustments before being moved out of the Shop to the outside berth for engine run-ups and brake tests, followed by final adjustments. In the foreground are what might well be the next two, D817 and D818 complete with chalked cabside cartoon. The latter two, all but finished, were part of the exhibition held for the naming of 92220 EVENING STAR on 18 March 1960.

Below. More Warships early in 1960. Steam locos in the background include 5024 CAREW CASTLE and there were further Warships under construction beyond. Around a dozen of the new diesels would be under construction at any one time in the works during this period.

2. The SWINDON WARSHIPS

TRAVAILS
It shouldn't happen to a Warship!

This volume is of course concerned with the Swindon-built B-B Warships D800-D832 and D866-D870. The whole class, however, was treated by BR as one (more or less) so in charting their fortunes the following brief notes encompass the North British examples D833-D865 too.

Except for the Paxman-engined D830 MAJESTIC, allocated to Newton Abbot, all the Warships, of all three stripes, Swindon and NBL and the D600s, went first to Laira, housed initially in part of the steam straight shed screened off for diesels and then in the new modern servicing shed and the splendid glass and concrete 'Maintenance Hall' – without doubt the best-looking diesel depot ever built in this country, by a long way. Surely it is listed by now? The period of the Warship ascendency, which had begun to falter even before the final delivery of D865 in June 1962, was brief in the extreme. From first rank express working, in little more than a decade they could be found trundling around, often in abominable condition, on all manner of low grade work. It is chastening to reflect that the Britannia Pacifics, for instance, did rather better! The class in fact was not confined to top duties from the first like say, the Deltics, nor were they put to a revolutionary timetable after the fashion of the Eastern Region D200s on the GE and the GN sections. The earliest Warships instead could be found on china clay empties and two coach locals. The locos followed steam diagramming to 1962 though that summer was marked by accelerations with an hour knocked off the North West-South West services.

In a most unexpected turn of events, that would have fair stupefied those wrestling with the mysteries of stressed skin welding techniques at Swindon back in 1958 and at North British a year after, the Warships came to be used in place of Bulleid Pacifics on the wholly 'foreign' Exeter-Waterloo workings. Control of the Southern lines to Exeter and beyond passed to the Western Region late in 1963, with the mighty Exmouth Junction acquiring the unlikely code 83D under Newton Abbot. In early 1964 it was announced that the D1000s were to be moved to the Paddington-Bristol and Paddington-Plymouth services, displacing Warships which would release them for other duties including dieselisation of the Southern Region Exeter-Salisbury-Waterloo route and Bristol-Plymouth freight workings. Trials and crew training began in March 1964 with D827 KELLY and a 12-coach rake of empty stock. D829 MAGPIE arrived at Salisbury for crew training at the beginning of June 1964 and was replaced after a week by D819 GOLIATH. Three return trips each day were made to Basingstoke using a train of thirteen condemned coaches. Was this laudable economy or a reflection of the WR's attitude to its new possession? Full introduction of Warships (the Swindon variety) came on 17 August 1964. While at Waterloo the locomotives were stabled in the Windsor line carriage sidings far out on the Windsor side where they could be distantly spied. Sometimes they didn't seem to move a lot...

The Swindon D800s more or less monopolised the Exeter-Waterloo trains, with the intention of simplifying maintenance and crew-training; Salisbury drivers were the only ones with training on the North British locos; the latter were very infrequent substitutes and usually only when there was a failure at the London end, one often being available in the capital, by a quirk of rostering.

In only the first few weeks there were several failures, which in some cases caused severe delays of over an hour. The Southern, smarting from the loss of its main line, was not impressed and soon the WR was being blamed for its 'worn-out' locos, despite the fact that none of them was over five years old at the time. The December 1964 *Railway Observer* was not impressed either: *It is depressing to record little or no improvement in timekeeping on West of England services to and from Waterloo. Failures of the Warship diesels are all too frequent and the number of times that steam has replaced diesel traction are too frequent to record. This service is indeed a poor advertisement for modernisation.* At times the sidings at Waterloo looked like a yard for abandoned Warships. Throughout November and December 1964 the performance of the WR diesels showed some improvement but steam substitutions were still commonplace.

The story is wretchedness itself from thereon. By the perverse incentives of the time, the Region got an enhanced grant for *reducing* track and the old LSW line seemed perfect for this legerdemain. In April 1967 the WR began the work of singling the Exeter-Salisbury line leaving a crossing only at Gillingham. Come the inevitable failures in the Warships, delays could be horrendous. The line had been set up to fail, was the widespread suspicion. *The Railway Observer* was indignant: *Loco availability has improved little – one has only to look at the Waterloo-Exeter service to see what the Maybachs are like, more than one has been collected from Waterloo and taken to Old Oak Common in July. On at least one occasion the 15.00 Waterloo-Exeter changed engines at Gillingham, a D65XX working to that point and changing with a Warship sent from Exeter – now a difficult proposition over so much single line.*

The Warships showed in a bad light over all this; unfairly, you'd think. The WR's heart clearly wasn't in its new line and the suspicion at the time was that the worse the line performed, the better the evil geniuses at Paddington liked it, for greater was the likelihood of its closure. Singling worsened everything. It's also hard to see how proper maintenance/servicing was possible (shades of the Great Central and steam locos here) for Newton Abbot was miles from Exeter where the Warships were 'based' (in a roofless shell) and in all the miles to Waterloo there was nary a fitter, let alone a depot.

It fell to D866 ZEBRA to be the latest Warship to disgrace itself, only days from the end of Southern steam, on 10 June 1967; taken off at Salisbury 34108 WINCANTON was 'hastily summoned' (in the usual phrase) from the MPD to rattle the train up to Waterloo in good time. It also took the return booked working from Waterloo at 5pm that evening. The railway press continued regularly to report failures and delays until Warship operation into Waterloo finished with the service handed over to Class 33s on 4 October 1971. The latter had been deputising for them on this route for some time, with failures due to broken springs a common problem.

The newly-electrified LMR London-Birmingham-Wolverhampton line had taken over the through traffic to the West Midlands in 1967, leaving the Paddington-Bicester-Birmingham route with only intermediate traffic. The North British Warships were to work freight and passenger services, allocated to Old Oak, though Tyseley and Bescot would carry out examinations and minor repairs – very different to the arrangements on the Exeter line for instance! In June 1967 D833 and D846 went to Bescot and Tyseley, respectively, for crew training. Four more were temporarily allocated: D834 to Wolverhampton, D835 Bescot, D836 Banbury and D837 Tyseley. Twenty-one North British examples were transferred to Old Oak Common between July and October 1967 for the full service, which only got underway in October 1967.

Reprising events on the LSWR section, by late October 1967 six Warships were lined up at Bescot having failed. Their unreliability forced a decision to restore Brush Type 4s to the Paddington-Birmingham services from 20 November barely a month later. Removed from the Birmingham passenger services, it was thought the Old Oak NBL Warships (eight of them at least) could replace Brush Type 4s on the London-Cheltenham/Worcester/Hereford services from the start of 1968. Inevitably delayed, two more Newton Abbot NBL Warships had to be transferred before the service could be got underway in the first months of 1968.

The Swindon-built locos raised some eyebrows when the WR began employing them in pairs on the principal West of England services for an accelerated timetable in May 1968. Twin Warships could maintain any schedule permitted by weight and speed restriction. During March/April 1968 trials were conducted with the first pair refitted with multiple working equipment, D824 and D825, in preparation for the new timetable. The official launch was on 6 May when D831 MONARCH and D819 GOLIATH took the first six hour Cornish Riviera as far as Plymouth where they handed over to a Western for the final leg to Penzance. Four pairs of D800s were needed to cover the accelerated services, working between London and Plymouth with only one exception each day when they went through to Penzance. Maintenance costs were high because each pair had a fitter and electrician and there was extra wear on brake blocks, engines and transmissions; the locomotives were refuelled at the end of each leg of the diagram. It was at this time that the Germans were said to have been frankly astonished at the high mileages being attained.

It didn't last long and from 5 May 1969 West of England services were limited to eight or nine coaches, suited to a single Western, although the accelerated nine coach Riviera remained double headed until May 1970; two of the four Warship pairings therefore ended with the new timetable.

The National Traction Plan, having seen off the D600s, was next aimed at the main fleet of Warships, Swindon and NBL-built; the latter would go first, then the Swindon ones. The three in the Pilot Scheme D800-D802 had already succumbed, after only a decade: D801 VANGUARD was the first withdrawal in August 1968 and D800 and D802 followed two months later. Unsurprisingly, the non-standard, Paxman-engined D830 MAJESTIC was next; after going into store in February 1969 it was withdrawn in March. There was not much time left; at the end of the summer timetable 1971 twenty-nine locomotives from both classes were taken out of service, rendering the NBL locomotives extinct. Only nineteen Swindon Warships remained in service at the end of December 1971. Final decline was underway; at the end of November 1972 there were just five left.

GREYHOUND trundled into Plymouth North Road with vans on Sunday 3 December 1972, uncoupled and promptly ran light to Laira. The Warships had sailed their last.

The Warships come to Waterloo. D824 HIGHFLYER with the 7.20am from Exeter on arrival at the buffer stops, long the preserve of Bulleid Pacifics, on 17 August 1964, the first day of the Warship-hauled service. This was doomed to be problematical; the locos were five years old and were launched far into foreign territory where they were not 'owned' by anybody. The earlier rosters of Warships to London took them to Paddington and often then to Bristol and back before return to Plymouth; all along the way it was a sea of hydraulic expertise in the event of problems but once a Warship left Exeter it entered a foreign land. J.C. Haydon.

The Western Region looked askance at these lumbering diesel electric locomotives, 10000, 10001 and 10201-10203 which carried so much weight compared to their power. There began a lengthy argument fought out mainly as a memo war (though it spilled over into the press) between protagonists, electric *versus* hydraulic. To the latter, it was a case of backward-looking lumbering diesel electric giants against nimble, advanced, more efficient diesel hydraulics. To the former it was proven worth against over-complex frippery. This of course, is to condense in a paragraph a lengthy period of argument and controversy. The trouble was, no slow, careful, considered programme of study, development and modification had been in place since the building of the LMS Twins and the SR trio. All had languished, getting older and stopped ever more frequently and there was little conclusive evidence on offer that could force a decision either way – it was quite possible to point to the prototypes and label them a failure, or at least obsolescent.

To take up the Warship story proper we go back, as with the Deltics (*Diesel Dawn 1*) to Germany. Recovery after the War accelerated in that country as is well known and very soon the 'Miracle' was underway. Early on a diesel hydraulic streamlined train had appeared and in the period when BR should have been nurturing its diesel future, the Deutsche Bundesbahn (DB) decided on hydraulic transmission for all new

PILOT SCHEME NOVEMBER 1955							
Type					Operating Region		
	Main Contractor	Axles	H.P.	LMR	WR	ER	Total
Type C	English Electric (D200)	ICo-CoI	2000	-	-	10	10
	North British (D600)	AIA AIA	2000	-	5	-	5
Type B	English Electric (D5900)	Bo-Bo	1100	-	-	10	10
	Birmingham RC&W (D5300)	Bo-Bo	1160	-	-	20	20
	Brush (D5500)	AIA-AIA	1250	-	-	20	20
	North British (D6100)	Bo-Bo	1000	-	-	10	16
	North British (D6300)	Bo-Bo	1000	-	6	-	
	MetroVickers (D5700)	Co-Bo	1200	20			20
Type A	English Electric (D8000)	Bo-Bo	1000	20	-	-	20
	British Thomson Houston (D8200)	Bo-Bo	800	10	-	-	10
	North British (D8400)	Bo-Bo	800	-	-	10	10
							Total 141
Power equipment supplied for BR-built locos							
Type C	BR Derby (D1)	ICo-CoI	2,300	10	-	-	10
Type B	BR Derby (D5000)	Bo-Bo	1160	20	-	-	20
							Total 30
Locos added soon after							
Type C	BR Swindon (D800)	Bo-Bo	2000	-	3	-	Total 3
							Grand total 174

building. It would be three years and the inauguration of its Modernisation Plan before the BTC determined on an exercise to evaluate the two types, hydraulic versus electric. In the meantime, it's interesting to consider that while the Germans took an avowedly diesel hydraulic path, in North America the diesel electric gained total sway. Who was to say at the time which system was 'best'? If time is a judge, it was the diesel electric.

It all began sensibly enough. In November 1955 the 'Pilot Scheme' was announced – it was some pilot scheme too, involving over 170 locos. Mr T.A. Crowe, President of the Locomotive Manufacturers' Association of Great Britain, issued a statement on the placing of orders for diesel locomotives by British Railways: *The British Locomotive Industry is naturally very gratified to have received these orders and recognises their importance as they are the first orders for main line diesel locomotives placed by the British Transport Commission under their £1,200 million modernisation programme. The industry has an impressive record of achievement as regards the design and performance of diesel locomotives for overseas railways and the manufacturers concerned are confident of their ability to provide British Railways with locomotives with which they and the public will be justly proud.*

The 'default' preference on the Regions other than the Western and at the centre, at the British Transport Commission (BTC) was the diesel electric. The Western took a different view, root and branch as it were. The Western Region people had contributed of course to the discussions and arguments during the gestation of the

D800, anonymous in grey on its first outing from Swindon, 4 June 1958.

D814 DRAGON runs out of Paddington bound for (probably) Ranelagh Bridge servicing yard or Old Oak on 23 April 1960. The diesels' impact was blunted for years by running them in steam diagrams. There was no real operating reason for instance, for a main line diesel locomotive not to head back out as soon as it could possibly be put on the next train, in the time it took to run round. However, stock was still taken out for cleaning/servicing at Old Oak in time-honoured fashion, the only difference being it was performed by NBL Type 2s instead of pannier tanks. In the meantime the Type 4s burbled away at Ranelagh Bridge, driving the residents mad, just as Castles and Kings had sat simmering for decades before. In this year, 1960, the simple 'A' was used as an express indication – see D816 and D817 later as well. ColourRail

The Torbay Express behind D801 GREYHOUND glides into Exeter St David's over the Red Cow Crossing in 1962, past one of the Z 0-8-0T banking engines, 30956.

SUMMARY		
Swindon Lot 428	TO TRAFFIC	WITHDRAWN
D800 SIR BRIAN ROBERTSON	11/8/58	5/10/68
D801 VANGUARD	7/11/58	3/8/68
D802 FORMIDABLE	16/12/58	5/10/68
Swindon Lot 437		
D803 ALBION	16/3/59	2/1/72
D804 AVENGER	23/4/59	1/10/71
D805 BENBOW	13/5/59	23/10/72
D806 CAMBRIAN	3/6/59	1/11/72
D807 CARADOC	24/6/59	26/9/72
D808 CENTAUR	8/7/59	3/10/71
D809 CHAMPION	19/8/59	3/10/71
D810 COCKADE	16/9/59	4/12/72
D811 DARING	14/10/59	2/1/72
D812 THE ROYAL NAVAL RESERVE 1859-1959	12/11/59	1/11/72
D813 DIADEM	9/12/59	1/1/72
D814 DRAGON	1/1/60	1/11/72
D815 DRUID	20/1/60	3/10/71
D816 ECLIPSE	17/2/60	1/1/72
D817 FOXHOUND	9/3/60	5/10/71
D818 GLORY	30/3/60	31/10/72
D819 GOLIATH	25/4/60	1/10/71
D820 GRENVILLE	4/5/60	1/11/72
D821 GREYHOUND	25/5/60	4/12/72
D822 HERCULES	15/6/60	4/10/71
D823 HERMES	6/7/60	4/10/71
D824 HIGHFLYER	27/7/60	1/12/72
D825 INTREPID	24/8/60	23/8/72
D826 JUPITER	7/9/60	18/10/71
D827 KELLY	4/10/60	1/1/72
D828 MAGNIFICENT	19/10/60	28/8/71
D829 MAGPIE	23/11/60	25/8/72
D830 MAJESTIC	19/1/61	26/3/69
D831 MONARCH	11/1/61	8/10/71
D832 ONSLAUGHT	8/2/61	16/12/72
Swindon Lot 448		
D866 ZEBRA	24/3/61	2/1/72
D867 ZENITH	24/6/61	18/10/71
D868 ZEPHYR	18/5/61	3/10/71
D869 ZEST	12/7/61	30/9/71
D870 ZULU	25/10/61	28/8/71

Modernisation Plan and one great plank of it was the wholesale introduction of automatic continuous brakes; implicit in this was that freight and thereby passenger trains too, would see a significant speeding up. For this sort of service, the highest possible power/weight ratio in a locomotive was deemed of the greater utility. Diesel electrics carried 'excess' weight which the locomotive effectively had to drag around throughout its life. Moreover, steam fitting staff, the WR believed, would more readily take to diesel hydraulic work than to the mysteries of electricity. Critically in the period leading up to the Modernisation Plan the DB introduced in 1954 what seemed an eminently elegant solution, the first five of its B-B 2,000hp Krauss-Maffei/Maybach V200 locos, weighing in at a mere 80 tons. It was this model that was in the WR mind from thereon, with the result that the place of diesel hydraulics was cemented in the Pilot Scheme. With that, the WR was set on the hydraulic path.

The Western got its way, just. Eleven hydraulics, Types 2 and 4, would be built for the Region by North British, which had acquired licences to build Voith transmissions and MAN engines. It was deemed politically too sensitive to buy direct from 'abroad'. Of these eleven locos five were Type 4s (they were to become the D600

Warships) and these were turned into 'honorary diesel electrics' because the BTC insisted on a six-axle heavy locomotive which at nearly 120 tons and 2,000hp, was a near enough equivalent to the English Electric D200 Type 4s being ordered. The high power/weight advantage offered by a Krauss-Maffei/Maybach V200 type loco was thus lost but it could be said at least that the BTC was acting in the spirit of the Pilot Scheme. A diesel hydraulic and diesel electric of similar power and weight could be assessed one against the other. For the consequent trials and tribulations associated with the D600 Warships, see the next *Diesel Dawn...*

To the Western Region, the North British Type 4 was a Trojan horse. The BTC felt it had got its way but the WR got what it really wanted with three further locomotives added to the Pilot Scheme in January 1956, to be built at Swindon utilising Maybach power-transmission-control sets. These were the scaled-down Krauss-Maffei V200 B-B locos the Region had eyed so approvingly while the Modernisation Plan was being argued and agreed between the Regions. There was the political problem of being seen to buy wholesale from abroad but the Germans had a solution; Maybach would supply the engines and transmission for the three

2,000hp locomotives. If satisfactory, a British licensee would be found to manufacture them.

Caution was famously cast to the winds from 1957 when the Pilot Scheme was overthrown; the pace of dieselisation accelerated with large-scale orders placed for locomotive types that were still on the drawing board. One major outcome to concern us here, in February 1957 was an order for another thirty B-B diesel-hydraulics to be built at Swindon similar to the three under construction. As it turned out, in view of the urgency the engines, transmissions and associated control equipment were supplied from... Germany.

Although overwhelmingly built in Britain, the diesel locomotive building programme that then unfolded was stuffed full of engines and transmissions with foreign names, to an extent that might have alarmed Mr T.A. Crowe, President of the Locomotive Manufacturers' Association of Great Britain quoted above. A curious absence from the list of suppliers was the USA and it has often been said that this was because General Motors (its Electromotive Division) would not grant licences. Yet GM *had* granted licences to build its locos (using US–built engines and electrical equipment) to Canada, Australia, Belgium and Denmark. The world's greatest diesel electric loco building firm and by far the most experienced, was frozen out of the UK on grounds of nationality.

From Munich to Swindon
The Swindon Warship D800 as we've seen was based on the Krauss-Maffei (Munich) V200 B-B locomotive. The major problem was to accommodate all the equipment in a locomotive 10 inches lower and 16 inches narrower. This doesn't sound much but was rather more difficult than it sounds...

The Krauss-Maffei/Maybach V200 drawings began arriving at Swindon in the spring of 1956. The Swindon Drawing Office Staff were faced with the monstrous task of getting all technical notes translated into English and all measurements from metric into Imperial. It does not take much effort to imagine the time-wasting and head-scratching when inevitably some dimension or other was mistranslated... Swindon had then to re-design the whole of the under-frame and superstructure to come within the restricted British gauge. All this, R.A. Smeddle, WR Chief Mechanical Engineer described in a paper to the BR (WR) London Lecture and Debating Society in February 1959 *involved learning and applying the aforementioned design technique evolved by Krauss-Maffei. The whole of the equipment had to be arranged on the drawing board into the new framework. The engines, transmissions and bogies were exactly as on the German locomotive, and it was decided to use similar engine control and compressed air brake* equipment. Most of the rest of the installation, including carriage warming boiler, cooling equipment, vacuum exhausters, windows, etc., was to be of British manufacture and this involved consultations, often protracted, with the suppliers. However, in due course, the drawings began to take shape and material was ordered. And then came the turn of the works. A manufacturing technique entirely new to locomotive builders in the Country, had to be learned and applied.

Instead of dealing with plates up to 1¼ inch. thick, bolted or riveted together, as for an orthodox steam locomotive, the whole of the construction here is of plate of wafer-like thinness, all welded together, the backbone of the structure being two steel tubes 6½in, outside diameter each running in one length from one end of the locomotive to the other. Such a construction obviously presented many difficulties to our Shops at Swindon, both as regards equipment and type of labour available. Sheet Metal Workers and Welders were at a premium and none of the Supervisory Staff had had any experience of the sort of work they were now to undertake. However, several visits were made to Germany and with the ready assistance of Krauss-Maffei, the first locomotive began to take shape, slowly and tediously, with a new lesson learned every day.

John Jennison writes in our own Irwell Press The Book of the Warships (2009): There was a very steep learning curve; Brown-

The pair from the other end.

Boveri personnel installed all of the 2½ miles of wiring in D800 as the Swindon electricians looked on. In effect, much of D800 was hand-built, creating the jigs for use on the later locomotives after they had completed the stressed steel superstructure for the first of the class. This was a difficult enough task in its own right but they also had to keep a watchful eye on its overall appearance with the help, or otherwise, of the Design Panel and its consultants.

The first impression of a D800 Warship gliding into Paddington amid scuttling pannier tanks and lordly Kings and Castles was a jaw-dropping one. Clearly enormous efforts had gone into making them look this good. The story goes back to 9 January 1956 when K.W.C. Grand, the WR General Manager, wrote to R.A. Smeddle, Chief Mechanical & Electrical Engineer: *As you may be aware the Commission have appointed Mr Barman to collaborate with the Chief Mechanical*

D808 CENTAUR outside the western end of AE Shop, nearest the Swindon-Bristol main line, for some final ministrations, 15 May 1960. These roads outside would be used to finish off odd jobs on locos coming out of the Shop – see D816 nearing completion earlier for instance. Locos would not be 'run up' (that is, started and left with engines running) inside the Shop because of exhaust fumes contaminating the air. Once engines were running, static power and brake tests were carried out, leaks corrected and so on. There were vociferous complaints from staff when engines were first started inside and the practice was immediately abandoned. This was not the first instance of fumes sparking revolt, interestingly enough; back during the 1955 ASLEF strike a number of condemned locos from the Welsh lines were cut up in the AE Shop to provide work. The smoke from the cutting torches resulted in a thick haze over the pits but this was tolerated as it gave the staff some work. Alec Swain, transporttreasury

Engineers in regard to the external appearance of all the diesel locomotives for which orders have recently been placed. *It is desired that he should also co-operate with you in respect of the three diesel locomotives to be built at Swindon. It is recognised that as these locomotives are to follow the Krauss-Maffei design as far as our loading gauge will permit, the scope for making any major alterations in the external shape will be comparatively small.*

Some months passed; the by now established leading architect and designer Misha Black (knighted 1972) and his Design Research Unit 'of 37 Duke Street, London, W.1', was asked by the Design Panel of the British Transport Commission to undertake this part of the work and he must have seemed an exotic figure to the inhabitants of the hallowed offices at Swindon. Steeped in the tradition of Brunel and Gooch, it is hard to think of any body of men more bound to look askance at 'outsiders'. Black had already had a part in determining the looks of D600 at North British. The overall look of D800, when it was eventually unveiled in July 1958, was owed overwhelmingly of course, to its strict derivation from the German Krauss-Maffei/Maybach V200. Black remained an influence through D801 and D802 going in service; he went on to be involved in the design of the North British B-B Warships D833-D865 and the Westerns.

Of the first Swindon Warships Black wrote in 1959: *In general they are making most of the amendments which we suggested but ... it is a fairly slow process as modifications are being scheduled for two locomotives or more ahead in the production series. Nevertheless the D803 is*

an improvement on D800 and I hope they will get better as the series progresses.

D800's naming in 1958 and inaugural exploits naturally proved highly newsworthy. The RCTS *Railway Observer* reported in the following terms: *On Monday, 14th July, the first of the Swindon built 2,200hp diesel-hydraulic locomotives, D800, was named* SIR BRIAN ROBERTSON, *in the presence of the Chairman of the BTC, Mr R. Hanks, Chairman of the Western Area Board and other officials. The ceremony was performed by Mr K.W.C. Grand. D800 had, earlier in the day, run light engine from Swindon and after the ceremony worked a press train of four chocolate and cream painted coaches to Reading and back. The following day it took the down 'Cornish Riviera Express' from Paddington to Plymouth with the normal ten coach load. On 16th July D800 returned with the 4.10pm ex-Plymouth with nine coaches (thirteen from Newton Abbot) including Saloon 9118.* D800 was adorned with a headboard

FIRST 2,200 H.P. DIESEL-HYDRAULIC LOCOMOTIVE BUILT IN BRITISH RAILWAYS WORKSHOPS – SWINDON 1958

despite the actual rating of D800 being 2,100hp – we had to wait for D803 for the first to be rated at 2,200hp.

Having made a splash already, the Swindon warships were now very much at sea, on active service.

During this period, another Warship, North British-built D601 ACTIVE had already begun work, during its own Diesel Dawn. More of this loco and its North British brethren D600-D604, D833-D865, in the following DIESEL DAWN No.3...

The BR Motive Power Committee heard regular reports on the availability of diesel locomotives. Through October 1959 for instance, with eleven and then twelve Swindon Warships in service, performance was judged 'generally satisfactory' with availability peaking at 80%. By April-May with twenty or so in service, availability did not dip below 72%, despite two at Swindon 'with defective engines', one 'still on special examination and two more 'stopped' at Swindon 'for attention to transmissions'. With all 33 in use in August 1962 availability stood at 80% with only two reported in works, for attention to their bogies. Laira had managed to effect two engine changes and a number of spring changes that month. For the Warships, it was now 'England Expects...'

Below. D816 ECLIPSE ready to run out of Paddington past the Arrival side box on 10 September 1960. From D813 onwards the nose doors had these four character indicator panels. ECLIPSE will run to Ranelagh Bridge engine yard to await the next turn, in well trodden steam working fashion; ditto the steam age red tail lamp. 1A33 was the 8.0am Kingswear-Paddington. **ColourRail**

D812 THE ROYAL NAVAL RESERVE 1859-1959 ready to depart platform 4 at Reading with the 11.40am ex-Paddington C35 service to Penzance, 2 August 1960. The name was the one exception to the strict alphabetical order applied to the production series (the 'pilots' D800-D802 were not in alphabetical order). To the left, the usual leg-swinging (can this be even *imagined* today?) gaggle of spotters is on platform 5, while on platform 4 three more compare notes. Headcode discs (was the top one *ever* used?) and simple steam age code mounted on the (equally simple steam age frame) before the conversion to indicator nose doors – this was the last one to appear with this old style framing. ColourRail

D800 SIR BRIAN ROBERTSON at Kingswear in August 1959 and possibly providing something a bit novel for the lads on the footbridge. The archaic combination of the 2-part hinged headcode discs and the number board frame, later replaced by the four digit route indicator 'roller-blind' panel is apparent. Peter Barnfield.

D811 DARING pauses for water at Shrewsbury on 18 May 1963. All the early diesels had such provision, for the boiler water tank to be topped up from existing lineside water columns and some indeed – D200s, Deltics say – had scoops to enable pick up from troughs. When columns began to disappear new rapid filling arrangements were made at places like this – a large diameter hose off the mains or suchlike. The round Swindon works plate stands out on the centre of the side skirt.

Looking black-liveried in the light under the Paddington roof, D805 BENBOW waits on 15 June 1959, at the start of the summer timetable, to leave with the inaugural run of the newly accelerated Bristolian. The train had been worked by a diesel for the first time a few months earlier, on 16 February. The schedule for the train BENBOW was working had been cut by five minutes to 100 minutes, the first 70mph schedules since before World War Two. The load on this down service was increased to eight coaches, the usual Monday 'extra' having been added. It reached Bristol in a net time of 91 minutes, in what was almost certainly the fastest run yet made from Paddington to Bristol, with a maximum speed of 95mph. Unfortunately these dazzling exploits were to last for only a few months before bogie troubles beset the Warships and speed limits were imposed.

D817 FOXHOUND new at Swindon on 18 March 1960; the occasion, with various locos and items of stock on show, was the naming of 92220 EVENING STAR. CITY OF TRURO was there, and KING GEORGE IV and EARL WALDEGRAVE too, along with D818 GLORY. The reversible train headcode discs had been abandoned since D813 with the introduction of the nose doors. The route indicator panels were then standard – the others were brought into line when in for repairs. RailOnline

D814 DRAGON at Bristol Temple Meads in 1960-61. By now a number of Laira diagrams covered not only Plymouth-Paddington but Bristol-Paddington too, the locos returning to Plymouth at a suitable point in the weekly working. Bath Road's steam locos were sent to Barrow Hill and St Philips Marsh early in 1960 while it was refashioned as a diesel depot. Diesels if needed could refuel at Marsh Junction, the new DMU establishment. It was envisaged that Bath Road would eventually operate 95 diesel hydraulics but it only managed sixty or more in the end. The shunter is St Philips Marsh's D3185. RailOnline

D801 VANGUARD at Bristol Temple Meads early on in its career. Based like the other Warships at Laira it was, like them, nevertheless no stranger to the Bristol main line – it would work up to London with say the Cornish Riviera Express, then do an early evening run Paddington-Bristol and late in the evening Bristol-Plymouth. In fact the first time the Bristolian was diesel worked D801 VANGUARD was the loco, on 16 February 1959. RailOnline

D819 GOLIATH in the period 1962-63, after getting its OHL warning flashes but before application of yellow panel. Chris Mills writes: 'The headcode 1V86 should be a clue, but this was one of those which spread its favours around promiscuously in its youth, before settling down in middle age to be the Newcastle-Plymouth night TPO. The only consistency in its early days was that all the trains on which it bestowed its favours passed through Bristol. With no emissions rising from the Teign Road power station in the distance this is probably summertime, when it would be on standby or shut down for maintenance. A gloomy day, but the light is poor suggesting fairly early morning. Two Warships (assuming one had not failed) suggests quite a heavy load for the onward journey over the South Devon banks and the train is pulled well up on the platform; enough room for 12 or more coaches. 1V86 covered a range of trains over the years During the mid-1960s and 1970s it flirted with various towns in West Yorkshire with trains mainly to Paignton, but these wouldn't need double heading. During 1961/62 1V86 had a brief Scottish liaison, the 18:50 from Glasgow combining with the 00:35 sleeping cars from Manchester to head for Plymouth and Penzance, due at Newton Abbot at 10:01. If that is the case we can see the carriages of the Glasgow portion at the front. The occupiers will have been fortified at Temple Meads, where the train made a booked stop from 06:30 to 07:15 to allow disembarkation to the station refreshment room for a full breakfast, there being no catering on the train. (That brings back happy memories to those of a certain age!). D819 will have come on at Bristol although an Old Oak loco was surely not diagrammed for this duty. Its compatriot may have been on all the way from Crewe; details of these night workings are hard to come by. One of the crew from the second loco is walking down the platform, perhaps to talk to the porter about to load something into the front guards van. Arrival at Plymouth was at 11:05 with arrival at Penzance finally at 14:05, a mere twenty one and a quarter hours after leaving Glasgow.'

D817 FOXHOUND and another audience, one member standing on one leg, at Paddington in 1960. RailOnline

The British Transport Commission very conveniently provided an educational leaflet which explained, as simply as is possible, the general operation of the diesel hydraulic transmission.

A special feature of the main line diesel traction scheme in the Western Region is the decision to employ diesel-hydraulic transmission. Although the diesel engine is very efficient, its characteristics (which are not unlike those of a motor-car engine) do not make it suitable for direct drive from the crankshaft to the driving-axle. It is therefore necessary to interpose an intermediate transmission which will convert the high-speed low-torque characteristics of the diesel engine into effective power at the axle. In the smaller forms of diesel locomotives, such as shunting units of up to about 200-300 h.p., it is usual to employ purely mechanical transmission involving an orthodox gearbox with power-operated change and some form of clutch—although even in this restricted field there is now a definite tendency towards a more flexible type of transmission. In the higher power-ranges, the purely mechanical form of transmission is not so suitable because of the heavy loads involved when starting a train, and the alternatives are either to use the diesel engines to generate electricity for driving the axles, or to employ a special form of flexible transmission. To derive full advantage from the diesel engine such form of transmission must be capable (as is electric traction) of affording infinitely variable conversion and effective control over the whole range of power output. In the diesel-hydraulic locomotive, the transmission consists of an oil-filled torque converter interposed between the crankshaft of the diesel engine and the gearbox (if fitted), or, alternatively, two or more converters are used instead of a gearbox. The torque converter comprises three basic parts: the centrifugal pump, or impeller, driven by the engine; the turbine or output member, fixed to the output shaft which drives the wheels through gearing; and the fixed guide wheel or stator; all mounted co-axially, and contained in an oil-filled casing. The input (engine) shaft turns the impeller whose blades force the oil (by centrifugal force) on to the blades of the turbine (fixed to the output-shaft) imparting a torque which makes it rotate. The oil then passes to the vanes of the fixed guide wheel which divert it back to the impeller blades. The oil is continually circulating while the torque converter is in use. The converter is so designed that the torque transmitted to the turbine rises as the turbine speed drops. Hence the torque converter is ideally suited to the well-known locomotive requirement that the lower the speed the greater must be the pulling power. It also provides over the whole range of engine power a smooth, shock-free drive between the engine and the locomotive wheels.

Two different types of transmission were used in the Warships: those built by North British employed the Voith system whereas Swindon used the Mekydro type. The NBL D600-D604 had the L306r model and the NBL D833-D865 an upgraded version, the LT306r. Both used three converters in conjunction with gear ratios to drive the output shaft. They had no fluid couplings and the change in speed was automatic through the filling and emptying of each oil circuit according to the relative speeds of the diesel engine and the locomotive. The emptying and filling was concurrent which meant that during the change there was only an insignificant drop in tractive effort lasting only a fraction of a second.

D800-D832 and D866-D870 built at Swindon had the Mekydro; this used only a single converter with four speed-change gears. The control gave automatic change whenever conditions of track speed required. At each change the converter, which remained full, was momentarily disengaged axially. The practical operation was due to the Maybach over-running claw clutch with automatic change, which had been invented in the 1920s for use in automobiles, and was developed significantly during World War II to absorb 1000hp. Unlike the Voith system, there was a complete break in tractive effort at each gear change, though normally this too only lasted for a fraction of a second.

D804 AVENGER on the up Torbay Express at Teignmouth, 28 July 1959. 'Diesel D Day' as *The Railway Observer* put it in 1959 ...was 27 July. This it turns out was the second day of diesel working on the train. During the preceding week those old favourites 5008 RAGLAN CASTLE and 5032 USK CASTLE were performing. As the up train starts its journey before the down, the honour of being the first diesel to haul 'The Torbay' went to D807 CARADOC. The down train had D808 CENTAUR.

Three character train identification, for the north of England. D810 COCKADE is at Dawlish with the 11.0am Penzance-Manchester on 17 July 1961, running past the as-usual fully clothed beachgoers.

A beautiful brand new D818 GLORY late in March 1960 at Paddington; this is the down parcels side and the loco could well still be running in. The multiple working fittings show up well, 'plug' this side, 'socket' the other. 3C07 was the 1.30pm Paddington-Plymouth vans, a regular running-in turn.

Numbers and Insignia

The Corporate Blue livery brought the double arrow symbol, which rendered itself so suited to an animated TV advert. On 27 October 1965 it was determined that all locomotives should have this symbol as a transfer, during normal repainting, 'one at each end on each side'. Many diesel classes received the new symbol before repainting in blue but not the Warships.

The BR 'D' diesel numbers familiar from D600 as early as February 1958 and on all the locos since, were termed 'serif'. These, it was intended, would henceforth be in the new, duller, 'Rail Alphabet' behind the cab door under the first window, rather than the cab side, where the new double arrow symbols would go instead. The first two to be repainted, D864 ZAMBESI and D831 MONARCH in October and November 1966, had the double arrows and numbers correctly positioned but the numbers underneath the window remained in the serif style.

The third to be painted blue was D830 MAJESTIC in December 1966 and disposition of the numbers/ double arrow was different entirely. There was instead a smaller double arrow above each nameplate and the

(still serif) numbers were (quite properly) under the cab windows with the Route Availability disc below as in the maroon livery. D846 STEADFAST appeared shortly afterwards with the same style and positioning as D830.

In March 1967 it was agreed that 'both symbol and number' should be placed on the cab side. Variations number/ symbol/route disc continued to sprout forth. From June 1967 some sort of continuity was imposed – the red discs were to be placed below the access panels thus enabling enough room for large double arrows on the cab sides. As it turned out, the original blue repaint, D864 ZAMBESI, was the first with this combination when it had to be repaired after a collision.

The 'Rail Alphabet' numbers at last began appearing in January 1968, when D821 GREYHOUND and D826 JUPITER were returned to traffic with 'Rail Alphabet' 'D' numbers with double arrows below. Following the end of steam the 'D' was dropped in October 1968 on 856 TROJAN and in November on 825 INTREPID.

There was a bit more juggling to come. Later in 1968 the BR symbol and loco number were repositioned with a TOPS data panel in place of the red RA disc on 803 ALBION. The final change, from January 1969 involved moving the symbol and data panels; 816 ECLIPSE

in February 1969 got the double arrow below the nameplate so the data panel could be positioned below the number.

There is far more detail available, into the realms of the mind-boggling. Take just this tiny extract from *The Book of the Warships* (John Jennison, Irwell Press, 2009): *Although the 'D'-prefix was painted out on many WR locomotives with metal numbers before they were painted blue, only one Warship, 852 TENACIOUS, had this done whilst in green livery, around October 1968. There is also no evidence that any maroon or serif numbered blue locomotive was similarly dealt with at this time. However when 826, which had previously had Rail Alphabet numbers and D-prefix, and 868, with serif numbers and D-prefix, were repainted at Laira in 1971, they both received serif numbers without D-prefixes. Their double arrows below the numbers were also replaced by single hand-painted symbols under the nameplates; and to cap it all, the numbers on 826 were not even level when applied! None of the class received TOPS numbers in view of their imminent withdrawal by the time these were introduced.*

D805 BENBOW runs into No.5 platform at Reading General. The original route indicator frame carries the steam-issue indicating numbers; it could well indicate a morning train up from Taunton. Gresley coach second in line behind BENBOW with a Southern mogul in the distance. The top disc (always closed) sat incongruously on the sleek 'V200' front while the middle bottom one for obvious reasons stayed firmly 'closed'. D.C. Ovenden, ColourRail

Three month old D813 DIADEM leaving the parcels depot at Paddington on 29 March 1960; this was a Saturday and indeed C11 around this period was the 00.35 SO Paddington-Penzance. The 4 indicated the type of train (1=express) in this case a fitted freight.

D816 ECLIPSE only a few months old, comes into Reading General with 1A41 The Mayflower, 8.30am from Plymouth on 2 August 1960. A curious steam leftover is the inspection pit at end of Platform 4; it was once *de rigueur* to examine and oil during a journey but was presumably not routine by this late period. ColourRail

The advent of the yellow panel and The Curious Case of 1MO6. Here we have D825 INTREPID, new in August 1960 and adorned first with electrification warning flashes in late 1961, then with the first modest yellow panel in March 1963, on 1 April 1963. 1MO6 was the 11.40am Penzance-Crewe Perishables for which thoughts turn to broccoli yet, plainly, the vehicles in this train will carry no trace of the prized vegetable, something of a luxury back then. Perhaps the April First date is significant... With the loco newly painted and more importantly, clean, all the front end detail is clear for once especially the multiple working equipment taken off in 1965 only to be reinstated in 1968 for the brief time of the double-headed West of England service. Someone has not noticed that the steam heating hose is hanging down unsecured. Note slot for Driver's name below window (never used) and the four sand box filler points at the base of the body sides.

The Curious Case of 1MO6 again, at Penzance now on 1 April 1963. Being a Swindon Warship, the exhaust ports (circular, one each end behind the cabs, are (with the exception of D830 which had off-set ports for its Paxman engines) in line; the NBL ones had them off-set – see *Diesel Dawn* No.3. Note the little rectangular flaps on the roof – these were simple ventilators and could look quite strange when all of them were open. These were simple enough, individually hand operated using a ring welded to the lid and fixed – and ultimately seized – in position. Note walkways across the radiator fans and abundant sprinkling of overhead line warning flashes.

D825 INTREPID with 1MO6 up again, 1 April 1963. The Pullman Camping Coach off to the left suggests the location is Marazion, within sight of St Michaels Mount. Both Swindon and NBL locomotives had that small oval vertical grill just outside the top right of the reporting numbers, as you look at the front. This was an air intake (not the horn as often stated) that went back to the German V200 design; the circular grills for the horns are under each buffer. The air intake grill is not painted over here – it was subsequently, when such niceties were no longer observed. Electric marker lights, one red one white. The 'plug' and the 'socket' of the multiple working equipment shows to particular advantage. Note steam age (Great Western 'side-on') lamp irons. Design gurus like Misha Black must have groaned at those two clips/butterfly nuts dangling idly either side of the top lamp iron; these helped to secure the (again steam age) train headboards which sat primarily on that top iron. They gradually disappeared; first the brackets, the fixings. It is worth noting too, that in order to change the roller blinds inside those doors, they had to opened from outside; that is, the Fireman had to get down at track level amid all that dirt and grease. This was unlike other BR main line classes and was not appreciated in the least. Note also that the locos had a 'bash plate' welded on to prevent damage from the swinging screw coupling.

D829 under construction with another alongside, probably D830. This would probably be about September 1960; on a visit on 6 November it was noted that D829 and D830 were 'complete' in A Shop, D831 and D832 had engines fitted and frames/bodywork had appeared for the final Lot, D866-D870. The first three Westerns, D1000-D1002 were also beginning to materialise. As it was, D829 MAGPIE entered traffic later that month but D830 was not ready, despite being observed as 'complete', until January 1961. NORTH STAR presides as ever.

D822 HERCULES under repair at Swindon on 30 March 1962. Hymek D7026 has newly arrived from Manchester and the Foreman figure (it looks cold in the shop) is guiding some heavy equipment alongside, by the look of it.

'Designed with a view to complete reliability and durability'
The BR Official Technical Description (greatly condensed) was duly issued for the occasion of D800's entry into traffic. 'Some brief particulars':

Diesel Engines (2 per loco.)	Maybach MD 650 Vee-type turbo-pressure charged
Rated Output per engine	1056 b.h.p. at 1400 r.p.m. (First three locos D800-D802)
	1152 b.h.p. at 1530 r.p.m. (Subsequent locos.)
Cycle	Four-stroke
Number of Cylinders per engine	12
Cylinder Bore	185 mm. (7.283 in.)
Piston Stroke	200 mm. (7.874 in.)
Valves per Cylinder	3 inlet 3 exhaust
Supercharger	Maybach
Injectors	L'Orange
Main Bearings	Roller
Big End Bearings	Plain
Fuel Consumption (Approx.)	.375 Ib./b.h.p.hr
Lubricating Oil Consumption	1.5 - 2 gr./b.h.p.hr
Weight per engine	10,250 Ib.
Transmissions (2 per loco.)	Mekydro Type K 104
Maximum Rating of each	966 h.p. at 1400 r.p.m. input
	1035 h.p. at 1530 r.p.m. input
Number of Gears (forward and reverse)	Four
Final Drive	Maybach type C. 33
Electrical Control System	Brown Boveri
Cooling System	
Radiator Unit	
Hydraulic Fan Drive	
	Serck Radiators Ltd.
	Serck-Behr.
Brake Equipment	Laycock Ltd.
Type	Laycock-Knorr vacuum controlled straight air brake
Air Compressor	Knorr type W 100/100
Vacuum Exhauster (2 per loco.)	Westinghouse type 4V110
Train Heating Boiler	Spanner type of 2000 lb/hr. capacity
Length over buffers	60 ft.
Weight in working order	78 tons
Fuel capacity	800 galls
Water capacity	1,000 galls
Maximum service speed	90m.p.h.
Maximum tractive effort at 30% adhesion	52,400lb.
Driving wheel diameter	3ft. 3½in.

Framing
Mild steel underframe and superstructure welded together to form one load-carrying unit. Two tubular members ran from one buffer beam to the other, to form the basis of the underframe. The superstructure had 'Z' cross section framing and other sections folded from steel plate covered by steel sheeting. The steel skin covering the framing was welded to it and to the underframe, forming a rigid boxlike construction.

Bogies
The bogie frames were also of all-welded mild steel plate. The body weight was transmitted to each bogie by means of brackets connected by pin-joints to the buckles of two large laminated springs. From these springs the weight is transferred through coil springs to the bogie frame, and thence by means of laminated springs to the top of the roller bearing casings and finally to the axle. There were no axleboxes and horns of the conventional type.

Engine

Two Maybach MD 650 type 'tunnel' engines, pressure charged by single-stage exhaust gas Maybach turbo-chargers. The engines had 12 cylinders in two banks in 'V' formation. *The basis of the engine is the one-piece cast iron crankcase accommodating the disc-webbed crankshaft. The roller main bearings are mounted on the crankwebs, the outer races being mounted in the annular walls of the crankcase. The crankshaft with the roller bearings is introduced into the crankcase from the front end of the engine; hence the designation 'Tunnel' engine.'*

Transmission

D800 had two Maybach Mekydro Type K104 hydraulic transmissions, each connected through a cardan shaft to its appropriate diesel engine. The reverse gears were contained within the transmission casing, the direction of change being controlled by electro-hydraulic means. If the reversing handle in the cab was operated while moving, no forward/reverse gear change was made until the locomotive came to rest. The final drive from each hydraulic transmission to the axle-mounted gearboxes was through two cardan shafts each having two universal joints – similar, again to those found on the V200s. The final drive gearboxes, 'type C33', were of Maybach design and construction. 'They are simple and compact and have been designed with a view to complete reliability and durability.'

Dynastarter

A dynastarter was placed in each nose of the locomotive for each engine, driven through a Hardy-Spicer cardan shaft incorporating a Layrub flexible coupling from an auxiliary driving flange on the transmission. When acting as a generator, the dynastarter supplied current at a maximum voltage of 135 at no load down to approximately 120 volts at maximum load on the first three locomotives; this was changed to a constant voltage of 110 for future locomotives. The current was used for engine speed control, supplying the various auxiliaries and charging the battery. When acting as starter, the starting current was drawn from a 56-cell lead acid battery.

Cooling System

The radiator, cooling fan and motor and header tank were supplied as a complete unit for each engine, placed into position through one of the holes in the roof and carried on a rubber mounting strip. The fan drive, cooling water temperature control and shutter actuating device were considered 'of particular interest, being the first of their type on a main line locomotive in this country.'

Brakes

There was a Laycock-Knorr vacuum-controlled straight air brake system, in which the driver's vacuum brake valve applied the train brake and made a proportional application of the locomotive air brake. By means of the driver's air brake valve the locomotive brake only could be applied. A 'Passenger/Goods' cock was provided in each cab by means of which, when placed in the 'Goods' position, the normal proportional brake application was slowed down. This was for use when hauling an unbraked or partially braked train, and prevented the unbraked stock from running into the locomotive or braked portion of the train 'with violence'. Compressed air was also used for sanding and operation of the windscreen wipers.

Train Heating Boiler

There was a Spanner boiler placed in the centre compartment. After the initial lighting up the boiler was supposed to be completely automatic. The working pressure was 80lb. per sq.in. The same fuel was used as for the diesel engine, carried in the same tanks.

D831 MONARCH out on the LSW main line and about to pass a Bulleid Pacific on a down working at Templecombe.

2. The SWINDON WARSHIPS

D800 SIR BRIAN ROBERTSON

D800 SIR BRIAN ROBERTSON	
Built/delivered	03/06/58
Into traffic - Swindon	11/08/58
Laira	09/58
Stored (Laira)	09/68
Withdrawn	05/10/68
To Cashmores Newport	18/07/69
Date cut up	By 24/07/69
4 character indicators fitted	24/03/64
Green	03/06/58
OHL flashes; serif 'D'-prefix	11/12/61
Yellow warning panels	01/05/63
Maroon	-
Blue	-
Recorded mileage	923,870

Shock of the New. D800 SIR BRIAN ROBERTSON during mid-July 1958 when it bore the headboard FIRST 2,200HP DIESEL HYDRAULIC LOCOMOTIVE BUILT IN BRITISH RAILWAYS WORKSHOPS – SWINDON 1958. Even though its actual rating was 2,100hp – the first rated at 2,200 was D803. The view is from the Teignmouth and Shaldon A379 bridge west of Teignmouth looking back towards the station. Mudflats of River Teign (not the sea!) on right; on left is Bitton Park sports ground and bowling green. Houses of Bitton Park Road top the skyline.

D800 SIR BRIAN ROBERTSON waiting to go 'off shed' at Shrewsbury MPD on 6 March 1962; it was a bit of an 'unknown quantity' and 7015 CARN BREA CASTLE was standing by as a precaution, ready and willing if the diesel failed. The man in the blue dust coat and trilby hat saw to that – Doug Sinclair, Senior Locomotive Inspector in the Shrewsbury Traffic District. In the early 1960s changes deriving from dieselisation had their origins a long way off, in the South West. From March 1962 the celebrated Newton Abbot 'double home' lodging workings from Plymouth to Shrewsbury went over to Warships. Brian Penney writes: *The new diagrams, when the Warships replaced the Castles on the 9.10am Liverpool-Plymouth and the 8.00am Plymouth-Liverpool services came in on 5 March 1962, with locomotives provided by Newton Abbot (NA Turn 1). This involved five locomotives on a cyclic diagram. Initially, on the North to West services, the Warships worked these trains between Shrewsbury and Newton Abbot, the crew workings being the original 'double home' turns involving Shrewsbury and Newton Abbot men (Salop Turn 102 and Newton Abbot Turn 154). These turns were single manned during the summer service. The first diesel hauled southbound train left Shrewsbury behind D811 DARING and the first northbound train behind the pioneer D800 SIR BRIAN ROBERTSON. Shrewsbury engine turn 50 was initially retained, showing the Castle as 'standby for diesel'. Until the introduction of the Warship workings Shrewsbury had an allocation of six Castles, 5038, 5059, 5070, 5095, 7015 and 7025, all involved in these workings. All had been withdrawn or moved away by the end of 1963. From 30 April 1962 the loco diagram was altered to include a driver training period at Crewe. With this alteration, on Day 1 the northbound loco went to Shrewsbury shed and left there to work the 9.50pm stopping passenger train to Crewe. Day 2 involved a driver training session on Crewe North Shed, leaving there early on Day 3 to work the York-Swansea Mails to Shrewsbury, arriving on shed at 3.30am. It then took up the normal working, 9.10am Liverpool-Plymouth, as far as Newton Abbot. Subsequently the diagrams did change and were worked by Laira Turns LA18 and LA20 in 1963. The Warship then worked through from Plymouth to Crewe and return. Crewe and Laira men worked the Crewe to Shrewsbury and the Newton Abbot to Plymouth legs but the Salop and Newton Abbot double home turns continued over the middle leg. The double home turns would have finished when the Brush Type 4s took over the Crewe to Newport leg, with Crewe men working to Newport. Regarding the double home working, the LMS had once provided an Enginemen's 'Barracks' hostel at the shed (close by the turntable – great for a good nights sleep!) used in company days to house lodging crews but this ceased to be used when the Western Region took over and by 1960 the building was disused and in a sorry state of disrepair. Both the Newton Abbot and Salop crews were happy to stay in private lodgings and were well treated by their landladies.* (From *Return To Salopia* in *British Railways Illustrated*, April 2019). Note the short hand rails below the windows – these were later altered to the longer version. Photograph Brian Penney.

D800 SIR BRIAN ROBERTSON with the down Cornish Riviera Express at Chacewater west of Truro on 16 May 1959. It retained its green livery until withdrawal. Michael Mensing.

A bit knocked about but still dignified in green, D801 VANGUARD undergoes the usual checks/adjustments including a top-up of fuel presumably, outside AE Shop at Swindon in September 1964. Four character headcode panel fitted in October 1963. ColourRail

Diesel Dawn

D801 VANGUARD

D801 VANGUARD	
Built/delivered	18/9/58
To traffic - Laira	7/11/58
Stored (Laira)	31/7/68
Withdrawn (Laira)	3/8/68
(Newton Abbot)	4/10/69
(Swindon)	21/7/70
Date cut up	By 24/10/70
Modifications	
4 character indicators	16/10/63
Multiple working cables and receptors removed	16/10/63
Green	18/9/58
OHL flashes	18/9/61
Yellow warning panels	16/2/62
Maroon - yellow warning panels	24/6/66
Blue	-
Recorded mileage	855,560

D801 VANGUARD newly in maroon, July 1966. Notes from Local lad Mike King reveal this: 'The train is a down West of England (well, just Exeter St David's by now as through services west had virtually ceased) just about to go under the "twin" bridges carrying a footpath just west of the junction with the Portsmouth line – just seen going off to the right behind the substation. By July 1966 the Warships were of course common on the route, having appeared some two years earlier. The carriages are mostly Bulleids, some of which were transferred to the WR and so got W prefixes, of the form W XXXX S. The prefix indicated operating Region, the suffix the Region responsible for repairs. D801 was one of the three "pilot" Swindon diesel hydraulics (D800-D802) and took some time to appear, whereas the production units (D803-D832, D865-D870) appeared from June 1964 and practically took over from 5th September 1964. Much, of course, to the dismay of all those like me who watched at Surbiton. Gone were those elusive 72A "cops" on the milk train at 4.20 every afternoon!'

VANGUARD leaving Reading with a Paddington-Paignton train, 1 June 1968. J. Binnie.

D802 FORMIDABLE	
To traffic - Laira	16/12/58
Withdrawn (Laira)	5/10/68
(Exeter) for component removal	4/10/69
(Swindon)	21/7/70
Date cut up	By 11/70
4 character indicators	24/4/64
Green	16/12/58
OHL flashes	28/5/62
Yellow warning panels	28/5/62
Maroon - yellow warning panels	6/4/66
Blue full yellow ends – double insignia, serif and D	10/10/67
Recorded mileage	912,880

Right. D802 FORMIDABLE comes into Truro with an up train during 1959. It's in the original condition of the first three with the short hand rails below the cab windows and the framing at the front for the reporting numbers. Replacement headcode doors appeared early in 1964. Michael Mensing.

Below. D802 at Exeter St David's with an up train; its maroon garb looks new which probably indicates the year to be 1966. FORMIDABLE was the only one of the 'Pilot Scheme three' to bear green, maroon and blue liveries. ColourRail

Bottom right. FORMIDABLE in blue with the full yellow ends, at Bristol in its final livery, applied in October 1967; it was withdrawn a year later. RailOnline

D802 FORMIDABLE

D803 ALBION	
To traffic - Laira	16/3/59
Newton Abbot	8/67
Laira	5/68
Newton Abbot	10/71
Withdrawn (Laira)	2/1/72
(Bristol St Philips Marsh Jct	11/7/72
(Swindon)	29/8/72
Date cut up	By 6/10/72
4 character indicators	1/2/65
Dual fitting of BR/WR AWS	21/11/67
Green	16/3/59
OHL flashes	7/9/61
Yellow warning panels	1/2/65
Maroon	-
Blue full yellow ends – double insignia, serif, D-prefix	21/11/67
Blue full yellow ends – double insignia, sans serif, no D	27/12/68
Recorded mileage	1,220,000

D803 ALBION

Glittering in its new green, D803 ALBION comes round the curve at Crofton with a down working on 8 August 1959. The view is north-east with the train just having passed over Crofton Level Crossing – the Kennet & Avon Canal Crofton Pumping Station is seen to the left. One of the two beam engines therein is an 1812 Boulton and Watt which is the oldest working example of its type in the world. The canal itself is immediately to the right of the train but out of sight below track level. As for '410', this was a service which was a FO Nottingham-Paignton up until the summer of 1958 and a Wolverhampton-Penzance from summer 1959; that is, our period here. The alpha prefixes came in from 1960. ColourRail

Coming out of Cornwall over the Tamar on the 10.55am Penzance-Paddington. Road bridge to the right. Two white diamonds indicate refitted multiple working equipment.

ALBION in blue runs past the Exe at Starcross with the 8.50am Liverpool-Plymouth on 28 June 1969. The curious building is the ancient Brunel pumping station, a relic of the atmospheric system of the 1840s. Much of the chimney was removed for safety reasons long before and it was used by a coal merchant till 1981; hence the piles of the black stuff.

2. The SWINDON WARSHIPS

D804 AVENGER

Warship on the 'North & West' shortly after their debut on these trains, at Shrewsbury station in April 1962, with the 9.10am Liverpool-Plymouth. It had fallen to D804 AVENGER to power the first up run of the accelerated Bristolian in June 1959, before the call went out to slow the speeds of the locos while the bogies were investigated. The careful but necessarily amateurish rendition of the train code certainly detracted from the otherwise thrusting modernity of the Western's front line diesel hydraulics; a proper headcode panel was not fitted till 1963. ColourRail

D804 AVENGER with a down local espied from Lea Mount, high above the tunnels south of Dawlish station (in the distance) in May 1969.

D804 AVENGER	
To traffic - Laira	23/4/59
Newton Abbot	8/67
Laira	5/68
Withdrawn (Laira)	1/10/71
(Swindon)	By 7/10/71
Date cut up	By 24/3/72
4 character indicators	27/9/63
Dual fitting BR/WR AWS	6/11/67
Green	23/4/59
OHL flashes	11/9/61
Yellow warning panels	10/12/62
Maroon	-
Blue full yellow ends – double insignia, serif, D	6/11/67
Recorded mileage	1,206,000

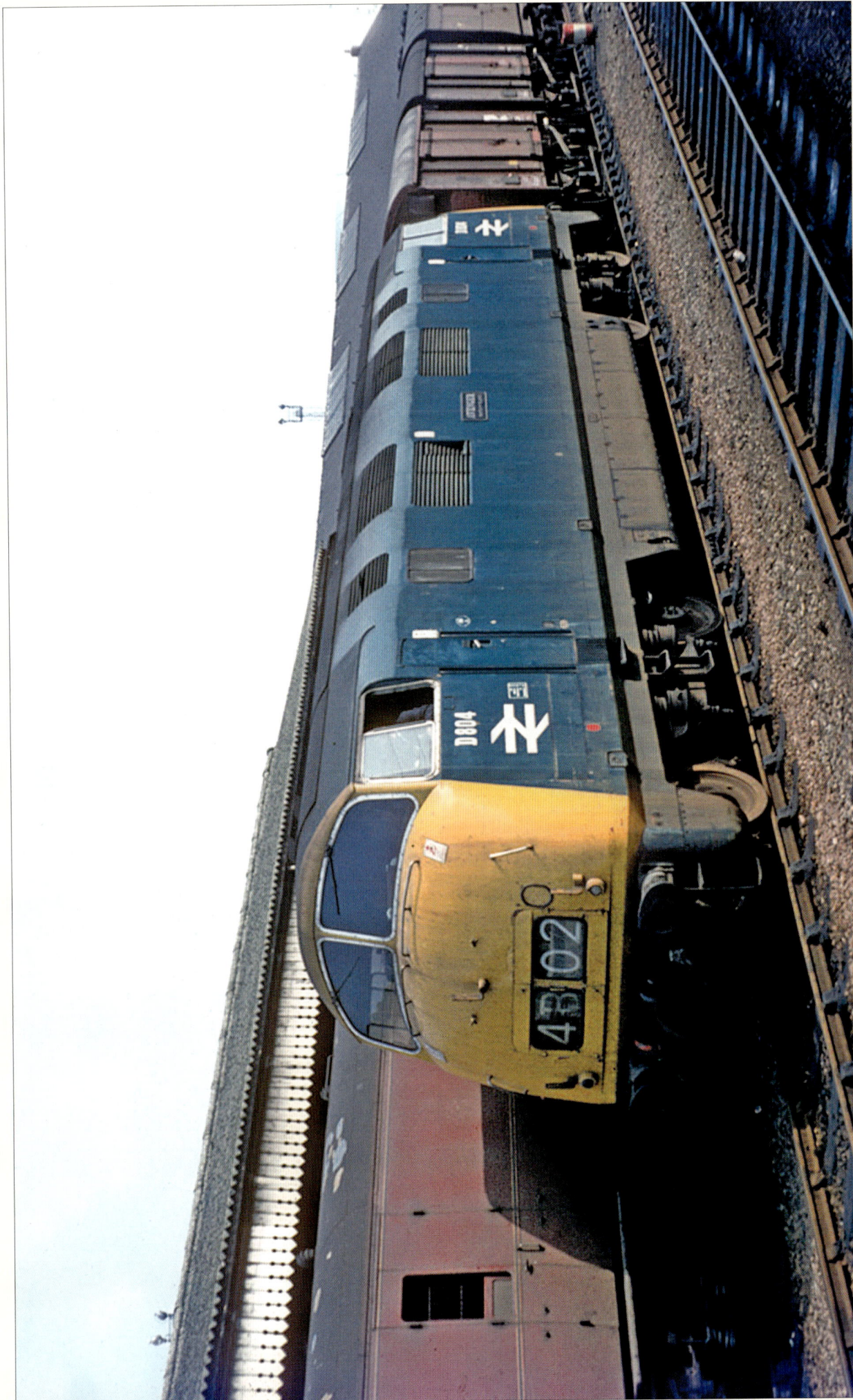

In somewhat straitened circumstances, a blue painted AVENGER finds itself at Gloucester Central with a Class 4 freight on 17 September 1969. It kept its 'D' prefix through to withdrawal a year or two later. RailOnline

Below. BENBOW at Honiton on 11 June 1967 with a down train, entering the station loop. The former up line trackwork remains in-situ behind the train, so the disastrous singling is very recent. Writes Mike King: 'That clump of fir trees on the horizon was most distinctive (less so today) as one came out of Honiton Tunnel at the top of the bank, on the north side. Not sure of the set number, but it is a mixed BR Mk.1 and Bulleid set. I think it is 3-set (ex-4-set) 873 strengthened with six Bulleids – the second coach is one of the 64ft 6in multi-door composites ex-sets 981-984. By 1967 to find a complete set still reasonably tidily formed was unusual on the Bournemouth line, but strangely those on the Exeter route kept their formations for longer. The Warships were Newton Abbot based in those days, but once the Cromptons were in use they struggled a bit and the train formations were reduced to eight coaches (nine in summer). I used to catch the 5pm down to Woking in the early 1980s and if there was a class 47 on the front I'd get home early; a 33 on the front probably meant arriving at Woking late, but with a class 50 there was no guarantee of getting there at all! The only failures encountered were with the 50s.'

Right 805 in blue at Exeter St David's on 8 May 1971. The code 1O10 refers to the 10.15am Exeter-Waterloo which it had worked the previous day.

D805 BENBOW	
To traffic - Laira	13/5/59
Newton Abbot	8/67
Laira	5/68
Newton Abbot	6/68
Laira	11/68
Newton Abbot	11/68
Laira	10/69
Newton Abbot	10/71
Laira	1/72
Withdrawn (Laira)	23/10/72
(Swindon)	31/10/72
Date cut up	By 16/05/73
4 character indicators	31/03/64
Multiple working jumper cables and sockets removed	7/1/66
Dual fitting of BR/WR AWS	2/2/68
Green	13/5/59
OHL flashes	28/7/61
Yellow warning panels	3/5/63
Maroon - yellow warning panels	7/1/66
Maroon - full yellow ends	2/2/68
Data panels	By 6/69
Blue full yellow ends – single insignia, sans serif, no D	24/10/70
Recorded mileage	1,281,000

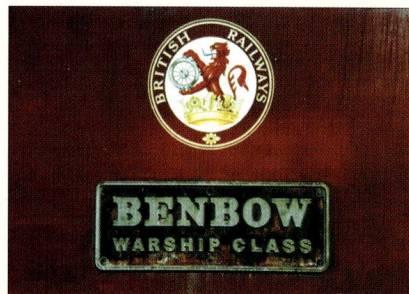

Below right. D805 BENBOW, Driver waiting, in a maroon world at Exeter St David's bound for Paddington (12.05pm from Penzance) on 10 June 1967; behind BENBOW is D1015 WESTERN CHAMPION, possibly a failure rescued further down the line and beyond is another Warship, also in maroon.

D805 BENBOW

Sparkling in new blue, 16 May 1971. This is Newton Abbot with the Diesel Depot, fashioned from the old steam works, off to the left. CAMBRIAN was withdrawn not much more than a year later.

D806 CAMBRIAN

D806 CAMBRIAN	
To traffic - Laira	3/6/59
Newton Abbot	8/67
Laira	5/68
Newton Abbot	6/68
Laira	10/69
Newton Abbot	5/71
Laira	1/72
Withdrawn (Laira)	1/11/72
(Swindon)	7/12/72
Date cut up	By 1/5/75
4 character indicators	18/10/63
Multiple working jumper cables and sockets removed	28/6/66
Dual fitting of BR / WR AWS	16/1/68
Green	3/6/59
OHL flashes	13/9/61
Yellow warning panels	2/3/62
Maroon - yellow warning panels	28/6/66
Maroon - full yellow ends	16/1/68
Blue full yellow ends – single insignia, sans serif, no D	4/3/71
Recorded mileage	1,281,000

It's always amusing to note in these summer Dawlish seaside pictures just how few people are interested in the trains! Shocking. D806 CAMBRIAN is in original green on a down train Paddington-Kingswear on 24 July 1961. It has the cluttered GW-style train reporting number frames built into the nose doors and this time the train number has merely been chalked on – with loving care though.

D806 CAMBRIAN in 'shabby maroon' which seems to have been more prevalent than actual maroon, with a down express at Bedminster, Bristol, on 12 July 1969. It was still in 'shabby maroon' when the full yellow ends were applied, a practice which made for a sharp contrast for a period. J. Binnie.

D807 CARADOC

D807 CARADOC	
To traffic – Laira	24/6/59
Newton Abbot	8/67
Laira	6/68
Newton Abbot	5/71
Laira	1/72
Withdrawn (Laira)	26/9/72
(Swindon)	5/10/72
Date cut up	By 3/11/72
Modifications	
4 character indicators	17/2/65
Dual fitting of BR / WR AWS	6/11/67
Green	24/6/59
OHL flashes	9/12/61
Yellow warning panels	18/4/63
Maroon	-
Blue full yellow ends – double insignia, serif, D-prefix	6/11/67
Blue full yellow ends – single insignia, sans serif, no D	6/10/70
Recorded mileage	1,317,000

807 CARADOC resplendent in blue in front of the marvellously extravagant fuelling/servicing shed at Bristol Bath Road Diesel Depot, 4 May 1971; 'final' livery arrangements with 'Rail Alphabet' number without the 'D', data panel below, shed code to right of Driver's door, double arrow beneath nameplate. J. Binnie.

D808 CENTAUR

D808 CENTAUR	
To traffic - Laira	08/07/59
Newton Abbot	08/67
Laira	09/68
Newton Abbot	05/71
Withdrawn (Newton Abbot)	03/10/71
(Bristol St Philips Marsh Jct	20/10/71
(Swindon)	06/01/72
Date cut up	By 25/02/72
4 character indicators	12/64
Dual fitting of BR/ WR AWS	12/67
Green	08/07/59
OHL flashes	30/09/61
Yellow warning panels	09/03/62
Full yellow ends	12/67
Maroon	-
Blue full yellow ends – double insignia, sans serif, D-prefix	07/68
Blue full yellow ends – single insignia, sans serif, no D	19/06/70
Recorded mileage	1,238,000

D808 CENTAUR with a down working at Weston Super Mare on 25 January 1962; it would shortly get the yellow panels. A pannier tank lurks in the background. ColourRail

D808 CENTAUR in scruffy green on the 5.0pm Waterloo-Exeter train passing through Wimbledon in June 1967. On the left is the milk dock siding and platform (long since abandoned for that purpose) which by 1967 was used as an occasional refuge for a goods train (as here) or parcels vans. It is mid or late afternoon, so the train might be the 3pm or 5pm down. Take in the selection of stock and liveries: BR Mk 1 brake second in blue and grey, two Bulleids in green, another Mk 1 brake but in maroon, followed by another Bulleid, BR catering vehicle and other Bulleids, all in green. Brake van in foreground is a Southern 'pillbox' in grey. Wimbledon B box just seen at right.

808 at Exeter St David's on 31 July 1971 bearing the familiar 1O10 referring to the 10.15am Exeter-Waterloo. A Western stands on the right; it was not unknown for one to substitute on the Waterloo trains should a Warship fail in Exeter at the last minute. It was highly unlikely/impossible that it would reach London however; almost the only hydraulics other than Warships to be seen anywhere near town were occasional Hymeks, especially on a Sunday when the down milk empties still ran via Salisbury – the only day of the week that this continued after 7 September 1964. This was usually a Hymek duty and the loco would come up on a late Sunday morning train.

D809 CHAMPION

D809 CHAMPION	
To traffic - Laira	19/8/59
Newton Abbot	8/67
Withdrawn (Old Oak Common)	3/10/71
(Laira)	16/6/72
(Bristol St Philips Marsh Jct	11/7/72
(Swindon)	29/8/72
Date cut up	By 6/10/72
Modifications	
4 character indicators	24/2/64
Multiple working jumper cables and sockets removed	4/3/66
Dual fitting of BR/WR AWS	8/3/68
Green	19/8/59
OHLW flashes	4/10/61
Yellow warning panels	15/3/63
Maroon yellow warning panels	4/3/66
Maroon full yellow ends	8/3/68
Blue	-
Recorded mileage	1,135,000

Left. CHAMPION received maroon livery with full yellow ends in March 1968 and was withdrawn on 3 October 1971 when the class was taken off the Waterloo-Exeter services. It had reached a nadir well before that however, at Bath in May 1969 when it came through with up minerals, a thoroughly steam age leftover which only a few years before would have had perhaps a 28XX at the head. George Wood.

Below. D809 CHAMPION, its maroon livery in fearful state, at Exeter St David's in June 1971. The code might indicate a train to the Scottish Region but the S is hardly a definite one.

Below left. At about the same time – maybe a day before or later – CHAMPION waits at St David's with a more familiar destination code, 1O for Waterloo; in this instance the 12.30pm.

D810 COCKADE

D810 COCKADE	
To traffic - Laira	16/9/59
Newton Abbot	8/67
Laira	1/72
Withdrawn (Laira)	4/12/72
Cut up	By 26/9/73
4 character indicators	9/65
BR AWS	1/68
OHL flashes	8/11/61
Yellow warning panels	21/9/62
Full yellow ends	By 6/1/68
Maroon	-
Blue full yellow ends - single insignia, no D	6/4/70
Recorded mileage	1,308,000

810 COCKADE at Exeter St David's on 7 May 1971 after arrival from Waterloo. It had finally gone into blue with final version of number and so on the year before but had enjoyed the singular distinction for a couple of years of being the only Warship in green with the full yellow ends. J. Binnie.

LATER...

Thirty locomotives had been ordered from Swindon in 1957, before D800-D802 ever saw the light of day. Subsequent locos, as is so often the case, incorporated a number of modifications from the first three. A redesigned torque converter housing in cast iron replaced the original light alloy version and with other modifications allowed the engines to be uprated by 10%. A revised Brown-Boveri control system was devised which had the effect of making the control system incompatible with D800-D802 – these three could afterwards only work in multiple one with another.

D803-D812 had the same Spanner Swirlyflo train heating boiler as D800-D802. BR then decided in favour of the very different Stone-Vapor steam generator. D813-D832 were so equipped (as were the NBL D833-D865) but D866-D870 reverted back to a Spanner Swirlyflo type for some reason, perhaps confirming that there really wasn't *any* steam heating boiler that would work satisfactorily. In June 1961 D818 was fitted with yet another Spanner Swirlyflo to evaluate its suitability for use in the new Westerns.

Much pain devolved from the BTC decision to carry on with steam heating instead of electric heating when bringing forth all these main line diesel locomotives. Despite heroic efforts, at which the above paragraph only hints, the boilers fitted in the WR diesel hydraulics were no more reliable in the early years than those employed on other Regions. While they worked perfectly well in the instruction room or in rolling stock, the rolling, jolting, vibrating environment of the locomotive engine compartment proved too much for their delicate sensibilities. D870 was in fact to be the subject of a trial fitting of electric train heating but this was abandoned even while D870 was still under construction. The only visible sign was that the Desilux air horns were moved to a fibreglass cowling at the front edge of the cab roof to make space for the ETH jumper cables below the buffer beam.

The most noticeable external difference was the fitting from D813 onwards of four-character route indicators, set in the front cab doors, in place of the steam-style train number panels. From D813 too, the two screwed traps on each cab side below the floor level were replaced by pairs of hinged doors to improve access for transmission maintenance.

All had the same German engines except D830 MAJESTIC, Paxman of Colchester prevailing upon BR to try out two of its 12YJXL engines (they used the standard Mekydro transmission) with a view to installing them in future hydraulic orders. The only outward difference from the rest of the batch was the oval offset exhaust ports and boiler room ventilating louvres above the cantrail. They were satisfactory – at least they stayed in the loco until withdrawal.

810 COCKADE at Bristol Temple Meads about 1971. It can only be guessed at as to what is going on but from the position of the various footplate types 810 would look to have been just coupled on the front of the Peak (or maybe has just been uncoupled?) This suggests several different possibilities – either the Warship came up attached on the front of the train to save a light engine move or to assist the failed Peak or it is being attached to assist a failure/save a light engine move. There's plenty of steam coming out in a couple of places which suggests the boiler is working on the Peak but noticeably the boiler water tank is being filled (from that hose connected to the loco near the rear bogie) so it might even be that the Peak has been added inside the Warship because of a boiler failure and is having its water tank topped up ready for departure... Though why not completely replace the Warship? Nothing is really definite although with crew members climbing aboard both locos it looks as if whatever was going on has been done and things will be getting on the move shortly. 'My money' continues Mike Romans, responsible for the preceding detective work, 'is on 810 having just been attached to the front.' RailOnline

2. The SWINDON WARSHIPS

49

BOGIE BLUSHES
'A problem of Track and Vehicle Interaction'

By the summer of 1959 the Warships had developed an alarming tendency to bounce and buck when encountering track irregularities. The Krauss-Maffei bogie of the D800s and the V200s had a novel feature in that the space normally occupied by the bogie centre pin was required by the drive system so a link and bell crank system provided instead for the movement normally carried around the centre pin. Such an arrangement, relying on deflection in rubber bushes and other wonders, provided for the lateral freedom traditional and necessary in a bogie. Or did it? There had been misgivings at Swindon but with no such problems manifest in the German experience all was presumed to be well. It turned out, however, that the DB V200s rarely had occasion to rise above 80mph, while new faster timings for the Bristolian, for instance, meant that Warships were being pushed to 100+mph.

Sam Ell, he of the steam locomotive draughting experiments fame and Head of the Experimental Section at Swindon, gave a comprehensive account in a paper to The Institution of Locomotive Engineers in 1966, detailing the 'serious troubles of diesel-hydraulic locomotives as a result of a fundamental error in bogie design'. Swindon's early misgivings were soon justified by two alarming developments; instability (which threatened to get worse when negotiating track irregularities) and sustained high-frequency lateral oscillation rendering the ride 'extremely uncomfortable'.

The problem emerged, Ell revealed: *...as one of track and vehicle interaction involving the lateral stiffness of the connection between body and bogie. Pending a solution of the problem a speed limit of 80mph was imposed on the locomotives and the tyre mileage limited to 50,000. Meanwhile the same design of bogie, extended to the C-C arrangement, was appearing on the Type 4 D1000 Class, providing an experience which was exactly a repetition of that of the D800 Class.*

Reduction of this lateral stiffness (was) effected by removing the Krauss-Maffei link and crank gear altogether, leaving control over the lateral and rotational movements to the swing links, which function then as in the Dean bogie that, in its time and for several decades, was a highly successful carriage bogie on the former Great Western Railway.

Proving trials were made over a long length of track in both directions in order to obtain a fully representative range of track and vehicle interaction. All bogies of the D800 and D1000 Classes were then modified and with the modification the speed restriction was removed.

Ell, who obviously had a sense of humour and having safely retired from BR, concluded his paper thus: *...the support of the body in the original design is made through a deep rubber block. Preceptors of old advised us what happens to houses built on sand, and on rock but, because the material had not then been invented, they could not advise us what happens to a house which is built on rubber stilts. This momentous discovery was left to British Railways. Hence the replacement of the rubber with a metal block and the end of the troubles with Krauss-Maffei bogies due to 'under-design.'*

Troubles with 'bogies and boilers' as we've now seen, did Warship availability figures no good at all. Neither of these sets of travails, we can further note, derived from the original Swindon work of translating the V200 into the Warship; steam heating was mistakenly imposed from above, the K-M bogie taken on trust.

D811 DARING with the down Torbay Express at Westbury on 28 April 1962.

D811 DARING

D811 DARING	
To traffic - Laira	14/10/59
Newton Abbot	8/67
Withdrawn (Newton Abbot)	2/1/72
(Laira)	By 25/01/72
(Swindon)	12/9/72
Date cut up	By 13/10/72
4 character indicators	11/3/64
Dual fitting of BR/WR AWS	30/8/67
Green	14/10/59
OHL flashes	20/10/61
Yellow warning panels	29/9/62
Maroon yellow warning panels	5/11/65
Maroon full yellow ends	30/8/67
Blue full yellow ends – single insignia, sans serif, no D	9/1/70
Recorded mileage	1,092,000

Blue DARING at Exeter St David's after arrival with the 1 o'clock afternoon Waterloo train, 29 May 1971. J. Binnie.

D811 DARING with an up train, one of those lengthy workings threading the length of England up to the North East, paused at Newton Abbot on 19 August 1968. The green Warships had the standard BR emblem borne on steam locomotive tenders and tanks; it was replaced upon repainting into maroon by the carriage-type roundel. Headboard clips/mounts and top centre lamp iron gone. The nose doors with roller blinds were fitted from D813 onwards and the earlier ones when getting the doors lost the lamp iron and clips – well, most did. They were removed on D800, D802, D803, D805, D807, D808, D810 and D811 but retained on D801 and D804. D806, D809 and D812 lost the clips/mounts but kept the lamp iron! RailOnline

D812 ROYAL NAVAL RESERVE 1859-1959	
To traffic - Laira	12/11/59
Newton Abbot	8/67
Laira	1/72
Withdrawn (Laira)	1/12/72
(Swindon)	8/12/72
Date cut up	by 4/7/73
4 character indicators	27/1/64
Dual fitting of BR/WR AWS	9/4/68
Green	12/11/59
OHL flashes	22/2/63
Yellow warning panels	18/4/62
Maroon yellow warning panels	31/12/65
Maroon full yellow ends	9/4/68
Blue full yellow ends– single insignia, sans serif, no D	13/3/70
Recorded mileage	1,243,000

D812 fiddling with clay wagons at Fowey in April 1961; locos like these truly were 'mixed traffic', to an extent no predecessor steam locomotive ever was, though of course it was circumstances that compelled it to a great extent. In the old days you'd have a Castle on the Bristolian and a 2-8-0T on 'the clay' and all was well in the world. Now, in a sort of quiet revolution, the same locomotive could do both! ColourRail

D812 ROYAL NAVAL RESERVE 1859-1959

D812 ROYAL NAVAL RESERVE 1859-1959 at Old Oak a few months after entering service, on 23 March 1960. The last one built with the steam-style train number panels. ColourRail

Waterloo departure. D812 in dull weathered maroon during April 1969. Like D800 its name did not refer to an actual Royal Navy vessel; moreover (again like D800) the name was over-long, so the stirring WARSHIP CLASS had to be omitted.

D813 DIADEM

D813 DIADEM	
To traffic - Laira	9/12/59
Withdrawn (Newton Abbot)	1/01/72
(Laira)	By 23/6/72
(Bristol St Philips Marsh Jct.)	11/7/72
(Swindon)	29/8/72
Date cut up	By 30/9/72
Green	9/12/59
OHL flashes	21/8/62
Yellow warning panels	10/4/63
Maroon - yellow warning panels	11/65
Blue full yellow ends – double insignia, serif, D-prefix	5/7/67
Blue full yellow ends – single insignia, sans serif, no D	28/11/69
Recorded mileage	1,099,000

D813 DIADEM with the down Torbay Express Paddington-Kingswear, passing West Ealing in 1962. It was delivered with the headcode boxes/doors already installed and of course all the following locos emerged so equipped, leaving D800-D812 to 'catch up' as detailed earlier under D811. ColourRail

Blue DIADEM in final condition as 813 ('Rail Alphabet') with central double arrow symbol at Exeter St David's with the code 1O10 familiar in these pages, 10.15am Exeter-Waterloo. headcode clips have fallen by the wayside though the mounts remain. Air intake at front blanked off. As early as September 1967 *The Railway Observer* could report D813 as 'the first Swindon-built Warship to have borne the three liveries, green, maroon and blue.' J. Binnie.

D814 DRAGON

D814 DRAGON	
To traffic - Laira	1/1/60
Newton Abbot	8/67
Laira	6/68
Newton Abbot	3/70
Withdrawn (Newton Abbot)	1/1/72
Reinstated – Laira	20/3/72*
Stored (Bristol Bath Road)	4/11/72
Withdrawn (Laira)	7/11/72
(Swindon)	12/12/72
Date cut up	By 20/2/74
Dual fitting of BR/WR AWS	25/8/67
Green	1/1/60
OHLW flashes	6/10/61
Yellow warning panels	25/2/63
Maroon	-
Blue full yellow ends – double insignia, serif, D-prefix	25/8/67
Blue full yellow ends – single insignia, sans serif, no D	23/5/69
Recorded mileage	1,238,000

officially 01/05/72

D814 DRAGON with an express for the north, along the cliff line at Dawlish about 1960. ColourRail

DRAGON in latter-day blue with central double arrow, in the dreary confines of the old Exeter steam shed, between round trips to Barnstaple, 22 May 1971. D866 ZEBRA alongside.

D815 DRUID

DRUID with paintwork in diabolical condition. The date is given as 16 May 1971 and the location Exeter St David's; by September it was officially in store at Newton Abbot and withdrawn after a few days. It was one of a handful to retain the maroon/yellow ends with serif D number till withdrawal, though in highly degraded state. Behind, blue D826 JUPITER was if anything in even more deplorable condition. J. Binnie.

D815 DRUID in maroon at Newton Abbot on 8 July 1969. ColourRail

D815 DRUID	
To traffic - Laira	20/1/60
Newton Abbot	8/67
Stored (Newton Abbot)	29/9/71
Withdrawn (Newton Abbot)	3/10/71
(Bristol St Philips Marsh Jct)	21/10/71
(Laira)	4/7/72
(Bristol St Philips Marsh Jct)	18/8/72
(Swindon)	22/8/72
Date cut up	By 13/10/72
Multiple working jumper equipment removed	23/8/66
Dual fitting of BR/WR AWS	29/1/68
Green	20/1/60
OHL flashes	By 4/62
Yellow warning panels	29/11/62
Maroon yellow warning panels	23/8/66
Maroon full yellow ends	29/1/68
Blue	-
Recorded mileage	1,087,000

D816 ECLIPSE

A perfect D816 ECLIPSE at Old Oak Common in 1960. The solitary A headcode was a short-lived indication of an express working, subsequently abandoned. ColourRail

816 ECLIPSE in blue ('Rail Alphabet' number, central symbol and so on) at Bristol Temple Meads, 27 March 1971. White diamonds (one visible, one obscured) indicate the re-fitting of the multiple working equipment; air intake blanked off. By June 1972 816 was dumped at Laira and had undergone a most curious repair, presumably following a collision of sorts, resulting in a 'stitched' patch at the front. RailOnline

D816 ECLIPSE	
To traffic - Laira	17/2/60
Newton Abbot	8/67
Withdrawn (Newton Abbot)	1/1/72
(Laira)	By 23/6/72
(Bristol St Philips Marsh Jct)	18/8/72
(Swindon)	22/8/72
Date cut up	By 22/9/72
Dual fitting of BR/WR AWS	27/9/67
Multiple Working jumper equipment re-fitted	26/2/69
Green	17/2/60
OHL flashes	27/9/61
Yellow warning panels	23/2/62
Maroon	-
Blue full yellow ends – double insignia, serif, D-prefix	27/9/67
Blue full yellow ends – single insignia, sans serif, no D	26/2/69
Recorded mileage	1,144,000

D817 FOXHOUND

In maroon with the 'carriage' roundel, where else but at Newton Abbot, on 22 February 1970. J. Binnie.

FOXHOUND in maroon on a down train at Dawlish on 14 August 1967 in a view that also affords an appreciation of the massively cantilevered station canopies. ColourRail

D817 FOXHOUND	
To traffic - Laira	9/3/60
Newton Abbot	3/67
Withdrawn (Old Oak Common)	5/10/71
(Swindon)	15/12/71
Date cut up	By 10/3/72
Multiple working jumper equipment removed	9/66
Green	9/3/60
OHL flashes	14/12/61
Yellow warning panels	8/3/63
Maroon yellow warning panels	9/66
Maroon full yellow ends	12/67
Blue	-
Recorded mileage	1,078,000

D818 GLORY

D818 GLORY at Exeter in 1962. From this fine condition it endured a long lingering demise, dumped at Swindon and periodically raided for spares for the two preserved Warships GREYHOUND and ONSLAUGHT. The hulk, though repainted and looking fine, was finally cut up in the 1980s.

GLORY at Cardiff General late on in its career, in the last blue livery which it acquired from August 1971, at Cardiff General. It was withdrawn in October 1972 during which time if found employment at St Blazey; it was noted there in March 1972: 'The depot likes to keep a Warship for the heavy clay traffic workings between Boscarne Junction and Fowey.' ColourRail

D818 GLORY	
To traffic - Laira	30/3/60
Newton Abbot	3/67
Laira	1/72
Withdrawn (Laira)	31/10/72
(Swindon)	26/4/73
Date cut up	By 25/10/85
Multiple working jumper equipment removed	13/4/66
Dual fitting of BR/WR AWS	8/6/67
Green	30/3/60
OHL flashes	3/10/61
Yellow warning panels	18/3/63
Maroon	-
Blue full yellow ends double insignia, serif, D-prefix	8/6/67
Blue full yellow ends – single insignia, sans serif, no D	10/8/71
Recorded mileage	1,137,000

D819 GOLIATH

D819 GOLIATH	
To traffic - Laira	25/4/60
Newton Abbot	3/67
Laira	6/68
Newton Abbot	3/70
Withdrawn (Newton Abbot)	1/10/71
(Bristol St Philips Marsh Jct)	20/10/71
(Swindon)	6/1/72
Date cut up	By 3/3/72
Dual fitting of BR/WR AWS	5/67
Green	25/4/60
OHL flashes	2/2/62
Yellow warning panels	23/5/63
Maroon	-
Blue full yellow ends – double insignia, serif, D-prefix	5/67
Blue full yellow ends – double insignia, sans serif, D-prefix	24/3/68
Recorded mileage	1,125,000

D819 GOLIATH passes Dawlish Warren with the down Torbay Express on 24 July 1961. The numbers of cars speak of the ongoing demise of BR's holiday traffic. GOLIATH was to be one of the first into the blue livery, carrying (like D857) much smaller 'double arrows'.

Hydraulics at Shrewsbury; GOLIATH and a Western about 1964. It never went into maroon but was one of the first in blue. ColourRail

D819 GOLIATH brings the down Riviera into Newton Abbot over the Teign, 17 September 1960. G. Parry Collection, ColourRail

D820 GRENVILLE

Green D820 GRENVILLE rolls through Basingstoke with the 3.0pm Waterloo-Exeter in July 1966. Times were changing; the 11am (the former Atlantic Coast Express) then terminated at Salisbury and through passengers had to wait for the following 'Brighton' to continue westwards. At the time this was said to be WR spite and on a few occasions the train had to be hurriedly reinstated through to Exeter on account of the number of through passengers. BR 3-set leading but one of those sets with a Bulleid composite replacing the BR Mk 1 compo – sets 526, 536 or 556 are the likely contenders.

D820 GRENVILLE	
To traffic - Laira	4/5/60
Newton Abbot	3/63
Laira	6/65
Newton Abbot	3/67
Laira	1/72
Withdrawn (Laira)	1/11/72
(Bristol St Philips Marsh Jct)	8/12/72
(Swindon)	11/12/72
Date cut up	By 15/8/73
Dual fitting of BR/WR AWS	4/7/67
Green	4/5/60
OHL flashes	26/9/61
Yellow warning panels	29/1/62
Maroon	-
Blue full yellow ends – double insignia, serif, D-prefix	4/7/67
Blue full yellow ends – double insignia, sans serif, D-prefix	21/5/68
Blue full yellow ends – single insignia, sans serif, no-D	6/9/71
Recorded mileage	1,126,000

GRENVILLE in 'final blue' at Taunton on 28 October 1972 with the 9.55am Paignton-Paddington.

D820 GRENVILLE at Swindon after acquiring the yellow panels. Below the main body sides the cleaning plants could not really reach and this area remained the almost exclusive home of brake block dust mixed with spilt fuel. Right down by the buffer this end is the shed plate which would be the 83D of Laira.

2. The SWINDON WARSHIPS

D821 GREYHOUND

D821 GREYHOUND	
To traffic - Laira	25/5/60
Newton Abbot	3/67
Laira	3/70
Newton Abbot	10/71
Laira	1/72
Withdrawn (Laira)	4/12/72
Preserved (Didcot)	25/5/73
Multiple working equipment removed	6/5/66
Dual fitting of BR/WR AWS	11/1/68
Green	25/5/60
OHL flashes	4/10/61
Yellow warning panels	7/2/64
Maroon yellow warning panels	6/5/66
Blue full yellow ends – double insignia, serif, D-prefix	11/1/68
Blue full yellow ends – single insignia, sans serif, no D	18/8/71
Recorded mileage	1,088,000

D821 GREYHOUND (now preserved) at St Austell with the 10.0am Penzance-Paddington, May 1966; the maroon, as ever looked pretty enough when newly applied but it lacked 'staying power'. The old parachute tank alongside, at the platform end, undergoing dismantlement, is a sign of the times. ColourRail

821 GREYHOUND under repair at Swindon and resplendent in the latest blue on 16 June 1971. This was its most extensive repair taking a good four months and amounted almost to a rebuilding. It included attention to fire damage; it had occurred in the engine compartment and was fierce enough to damage the external paintwork.

D822 HERCULES

Honiton, and during July 1966 a green D822 HERCULES is ward to a maroon Warship, possibly rescued but (more likely) it is working home to the West as an earlier failure itself, in July 1966. The train is the 9.0am Waterloo-Exeter. ColourRail

D822 HERCULES in blue (double arrows each end) with up parcels at Horton Road, Gloucester, 20 February 1970. It was never in maroon. J. Binnie.

D822 HERCULES	
To traffic - Laira	15/6/60
Newton Abbot	9/62
Laira	6/65
Newton Abbot	3/67
Laira	8/67
Withdrawn (Newton Abbot)	4/10/71
(Bristol St Philips Marsh Jct)	20/10/71
(Swindon)	6/1/72
Date cut up	By 18/2/72
Green	15/6/60
OHL flashes	20/3/62
Yellow warning panels	26/1/62
Maroon	-
Blue full yellow ends – double insignia, sans serif, D-prefix	27/3/68
Recorded mileage	1,098,000

D823 HERMES, the only one to carry a vessel's crest (just visible by the number at the far end) with an up train (the 10.40am Plymouth-Brighton) at Honiton in July 1966. The Southern Railway more than once gave thought to electrifying its main line to Exeter but no one could have foreseen the queer 'semi-detached' fate to which it was eventually condemned, operated by a Region which regarded it as an encumbrance. The Warship regime on the Exeter-Waterloo line lasted six years or so and as 823, HERMES was one of those promptly withdrawn on arrival at London on Sunday 3 October 1971, at the end of that era. ColourRail

D823 HERMES	
To traffic - Laira	6/7/60
Newton Abbot	9/62
Laira	6/65
Newton Abbot	3/67
Withdrawn (Old Oak Common)	4/10/71
(Swindon)	15/12/71
Date cut up	By 19/5/72
Green	6/7/60
OHL flashes	21/9/61
Yellow warning panels	23/4/63
Maroon yellow warning panels	5/66
Maroon full yellow ends	By 5/68
Blue full yellow ends – single insignia, sans serif, no D	19/9/69
Recorded mileage	1,058,000

D823 HERMES

D824 HIGHFLYER	
To traffic – Laira	27/7/60
Newton Abbot	2/61
Laira	6/65
Newton Abbot	3/67
Laira	8/67
Newton Abbot	10/71
Laira	1/72
Withdrawn (Laira)	1/12/72
(Bristol Bath Road)*	8/12/72
(Bristol St Philips Marsh Jct)	By 5/2/73
(Swindon)	18/12/73
Date cut up	By 18/6/75
Green	27/7/60
OHL flashes	16/10/61
Yellow warning panels	31/5/62
Maroon	-
Blue full yellow ends – double insignia, sans serif , no D	23/4/69
Recorded mileage	1,077,000

* for possible use by Derby RTC

D824 HIGHFLYER

D824 HIGHFLYER with the yellow panels, entering Paddington in September 1964. ColourRail

824, one of the very last in service, running light at Bedminster on 29 June 1969. John Jennison has noted that the large central double arrow somehow foreshortened the locos; an optical illusion but real – if an illusion can be called real. Compare with side-on views of the locos, green and blue, *without* the central insignia. J. Binnie.

D825 INTREPID

D825 INTREPID has found its way to Weymouth shed (a BR Class 5 lurks in the background) on 20 August 1966; it was not its first appearance at unusual Southern haunts (for Warships that it) for it had substituted for a DMU on a Cardiff-Portsmouth Harbour train early in the year, working all the way through. ColourRail

825 approaching Dawlish with a short freight on 1 May 1971. It would be one of those Warships reinstated for a period after withdrawal which first came on 1 January 1972.

D825 INTREPID	
To traffic - Laira	24/8/60
Newton Abbot	1/61
Laira	6/65
Newton Abbot	3/67
Laira	8/67
Newton Abbot	10/71
Withdrawn (Newton Abbot)	1/1/72
Reinstated - Laira	20/3/72*
Withdrawn (Laira)	23/8/72
(Swindon)	5/10/72
Date cut up	By 27/10/72
Green	24/8/60
OHL flashes	11/12/61
Yellow warning panels	28/3/63
Maroon	-
Blue full yellow ends – double insignia, sans serif , no D	27/11/68
Recorded mileage	1,014,000

*officially 01/05/72

D826 JUPITER

D826 JUPITER	
To traffic - Laira	7/9/60
Newton Abbot	1/61
Laira	6/65
Newton Abbot	3/67
Laira	8/67
Withdrawn (Newton Abbot)	18/10/71
(Bristol St Philips Marsh Jct)	26/10/71
(Swindon)	30/12/71
Date cut up	By 21/01/72
Multiple working jumper cables and sockets removed	4/8/66
Green	7/9/60
OHL flashes	By 3/62
Yellow warning panels	30/10/62
Maroon	-
Blue full yellow ends – double insignia, sans serif, D-prefix	19/1/68
Blue full yellow ends – single insignia, serif, no D	7/7/71
Recorded mileage	1,097,000

Double heading an up express with D868 ZEPHYR at Reading on 1 June 1968. Multiple working apparatus was re-fitted to fifteen Warships from the summer of 1968 to work accelerated West of England services, indicated by the double white diamond symbols on the buffer beam. J. Binnie.

They didn't get worse than this! Looking like it has spent several years in a scrap yard, D826 JUPITER stands next to D815 DRUID (see also earlier) at Exeter on 8 May 1971. Poor bodywork like this has often been attributed to ill-judged use of chemicals in the Laira cleaning plant though the effects of this would presumably been identified and ameliorated after a year or two. No amount of washing could account for this level of damage. Worse was in store for JUPITER which 'caught fire' at Fenton on the 10.15am St David's-Waterloo on 14 May 1971; it had to be towed back to Exeter but the damage must have been slight, for it was not withdrawn till later in the year, undergoing several further repairs in the process.

D827 KELLY

D827 KELLY	
To traffic - Laira	4/10/60
Newton Abbot	1/61
Laira	3/63
Newton Abbot	5/66
Laira	8/67
Newton Abbot	10/71
Withdrawn (Newton Abbot)	1/1/72
(Laira)	By 25/1/72
(Swindon)	12/9/72
Date cut up	By 13/10/72
Green	4/10/60
OHL flashes	20/10/61
Yellow warning panels	2/05/62
Maroon	-
Blue full yellow ends – double insignia, serif, D-prefix	11/8/67
Blue full yellow ends – double insignia, sans serif, no D	23/4/71
Recorded mileage	1,071,000

D827 KELLY glides into Paddington in its first years. ColourRail

D827 KELLY with an up express at Bedminster on 29 June 1969. The eagle-eyed John Jennison detected a quirk unique to D827. In 1968 the electrification flashes behind the doors had gone missing. When replaced they appeared to the *front* to the doors, as here... A late repaint in green meant it 'skipped' acquiring the maroon livery. J. Binnie

KELLY newly overhauled outside the by now familiar Swindon AE Shop, in customary repose as it is tested and victualled ready to work trials and then return home. The period is probably May 1962, with the yellow panels newly applied. ColourRail

Diesel Dawn

KELLY now with the central double arrow, at Exeter St David's depot on 22 May 1971. Readers will note the difference in the positioning of the flashes compared to 811 DARING alongside... J. Binnie.

D828 MAGNIFICENT

Looking sleek in new blue – sadly it never lasted – in the wide open spaces of Bristol Bath Road DMD. J. Binnie.

D828 MAGNIFICENT	
To traffic - Laira	19/10/60
Newton Abbot	1/61
Laira	6/65
Newton Abbot	9/65
Laira	8/67
Stored (Laira)	13/7/71
Withdrawn (Newton Abbot)	28/8/71
(Swindon)	15/10/71
Date cut up	By 7/4/72
Green	19/10/60
OHL flashes	1/2/62
Yellow warning panels	9/5/62
Maroon yellow warning panels	By 6/3/66
Blue full yellow ends – double insignia, sans serif , no D	12/7/69
Recorded mileage	922,000

D829 MAGPIE

D829 MAGPIE	
To traffic - Laira	23/11/60
Newton Abbot	1/61
Laira	6/65
Newton Abbot	9/65
Laira	8/67
Newton Abbot	10/71
Withdrawn (Newton Abbot)	1/1/72
Laira	17/3/72*
Withdrawn (Westbury)	25/8/72
(Laira)	26/8/72
(Bristol Bath Road) **	5/10/72
(Swindon)	12/12/72
Date cut up	By 30/1/74
Green	23/11/60
OHLW flashes	5/10/61
Yellow warning panels	13/9/62
Maroon yellow warning panels	12/65
Maroon full yellow ends	6/68
Blue full yellow ends – double insignia, sans serif, no D	10/69
Recorded mileage	975,000

*Reinstated – officially 01/05/72
** for possible preservation by the TV
programme 'Magpie'

During the brief double heading period of the Warships, D829 MAGPIE heads D823 HERMES out of Paddington on the 8.30am to Penzance on 1 June 1968. Both are in the maroon which had come about in 1965 and by now thoroughly ruined of course (worse in MAGPIE than in HERMES) by penny-pinching 'patch painting'. The maroon followed that by-then familiar on the Westerns which in turn had come about through a competition. The WR offered three choices, desert sand, maroon or green; three hundred entered and the winner was maroon. The prize was a ride in a diesel cab but whether all those voting maroon got a ride or just one picked as in a raffle is not clear. J. Binnie.

Now in blue, 829 MAGPIE comes off the Brunel bridge at Plymouth with the 8.15am Penzance-Paddington train on 8 July 1971. J. Perry.

D830 MAJESTIC

D830 MAJESTIC at Crofton in September 1966 on the 8.20am Kingswear-Paddington; it was unique in the class in having Paxman Ventura engines coupled to Mekydro transmissions. The Colchester firm had persuaded the British Transport Commission to try out its high speed design, built with the purpose of providing a UK alternative to the German engines. The Paxmans were at a power disadvantage linked to the Mekydro transmissions which was unfortunate while poor performance by other of the firm's engines in Type 1 locomotives soured relations. Swindon Warship production came to a close shortly after MAJESTIC entered traffic and the Paxman engines in the event were deemed impractical for further use in the Western Region. MAJESTIC thus remained unique and along with D800-D802 was destined for early withdrawal. It had a reputation for above-average reliability but this was hardly surprising, when a Paxman boffin frequently travelled on board as a 'troubleshooter'. P.M. Alexander, ColourRail

D830 MAJESTIC	
To traffic - Newton Abbot	19/1/61
Stored (Newton Abbot)	2/69
Withdrawn (Newton Abbot)	26/3/69
(Laira)	By 25/6/69
(Exeter)	4/10/69
(Swindon)	27/7/70
Date cut up	By 22/10/71
Green	19/1/61
OHL flashes	9/4/62
Yellow warning panels	9/4/62
Maroon	-
Blue yellow panels – single insignia, serif, D-prefix	8/1/67
Blue full yellow ends – single insignia, serif, D-prefix	8/67
Recorded mileage	447,000

Crossing the mighty Taw at Bishops Tawton with the 12.22pm Barnstaple-Exeter on 10 July 1971.

D831 MONARCH

D831 MONARCH in a wintry world at
Devonport on 28 December 1965. ColourRail

D831 MONARCH	
To traffic – Laira	11/1/61
Newton Abbot	7/61
Laira	6/65
Newton Abbot	9/65
Laira	8/67
Withdrawn (Laira)	8/10/71
(Bristol St Philips Marsh Jct)	18/10/71
(Swindon)	16/3/72
Date cut up	By 23/6/72
Multiple working jumper cables And sockets removed	30/11/66
Green	11/1/61
OHL flashes	13/10/61
Yellow warning panels	17/1/63
Maroon	-
Blue yellow panels – double insignia, serif numbers positioned underneath bodyside windows, D-prefix	30/11/66
Blue full yellow ends – single insignia, sans serif, no D	4/3/69
Recorded mileage	1,011,000

D832 ONSLAUGHT

D832 ONSLAUGHT	
To traffic - Laira	8/2/61
Newton Abbot	7/61
Laira	6/65
Newton Abbot	9/65
Laira	8/67
Newton Abbot	10/71
Laira	1/72
Stored (Laira)	7/11/72
Withdrawn (Laira)	16/12/72
Derby RTC	10/1/73
Preserved	4/79
Green	8/2/61
OHL flashes	14/11/61
Yellow warning panels	1/12/62
Maroon yellow panels	1/4/66
Maroon full yellow ends	3/69
Blue full yellow ends – double insignia, sans serif, no D	11/70
Recorded mileage	1,131,000

Now-preserved D832 ONSLAUGHT with the 10.20am Exeter-Waterloo on 19 June 1965, on the Southern between Brookwood and Sturt Lane Junction, where the line to Frimley and Ascot branches off northward. The conductor rails are only on the local lines here and this stretch was at that time only used by a few electric trains running between Woking and Ascot – a couple each weekday and then on Ascot race days. Mike King, as ever, describes the stock: 7-set 703 formed in 1965 only comprising Bulleid semi-open brake second 4378, a Bulleid buffet car, a BR open second as dining accommodation, Bulleid corridor first (none of these have the coach number stated in the carriage working notices), BR composite 15568, Bulleid brake 4380 (wrong way round) and BR corridor second 24307. This set is tailed by a 3-set formed of two BR brakes and a composite in the centre. Sets 701, 702 and 703 were formed in 1965 for Waterloo-Exeter services (sets 701/2 were 8-coach formations) but apart from being mixed Bulleid/BR Mk.1 stock were also interesting in that one brake coach was not at the end of the set and had the brake end 'inbound' so as to bring the guard's van alongside the platforms at certain stations such as Honiton and Crewkerne, which had fairly short platforms. These stations were, of course, only served by local trains before September 1964, but after WR dieselisation got the benefit of through semi-fast services to and from Waterloo.

Its paintwork suffering as if from enemy air attack, D832 ONSLAUGHT stands on a road of the old steam shed at Horton Road, Gloucester on 29 April 1970. J. Binnie.

Another place where pannier tanks and Halls once stood... These are the ancient roads of 83C Exeter MPD, now a shell serving as diesel stabling point. It is 29 May 1971 and the loco is in the last blue livery. It was withdrawn in December 1972 following a period of some weeks in store. It moved to Derby Technical Centre in December 1972 and survival there made its preservation possible in 1979. Mike King writes of that curious tank wagon alongside it: 'Yes, it probably is one of the old GWR gas tanks. Interestingly, quite a number of these (and SR ones) existed to the 1970s, yet there were almost no gas lit coaches still running after the 1950s (the two ex-Barry Railway vehicles on the Hemyock branch come to mind) so just what were these things doing by then? There were always a dozen or more at Eastleigh so were they converted as water tanks? Or were they just sitting around until someone decided they were redundant and could be cut up? This one looks in good condition - unlike most of the former SR ones which were by then caked in grime and rust. Oil fuel tank wagon behind – presumably the diesel loco top-up arrangements. As Brian Penney has commented, this was always a bit hit and miss – the procedure used was 'fill to spill' as the indicator floats were notoriously unreliable and instances of locos running out of fuel were not unknown. This is why so many diesel locos were grime encrusted along the tanks – with muck adhering to where the fuel oil had spilled and run down the tanks. I saw ONSLAUGHT driven into the side of another hydraulic at Plymouth in 1970 – being driven from rear cab – siding collision only, but definitely an onslaught!' J. Binnie.

D866 ZEBRA

Sticky-out ears, short back and sides and bottle of pop so very much of the time, slightly obscure our view of D866 ZEBRA at Hereford in the summer of 1962, with the 11.0am Penzance-Manchester. G. Parry Collection, ColourRail

D866 at Swindon at Swindon on 25 August 1871 on the familiar 'test roads' outside AE Shop. Locos like ZEBRA were moved out to started up in the open and for various tests, brakes and so on, to be carried out and adjustments made. ColourRail

D866 ZEBRA	
To traffic - Laira	24/03/61
Newton Abbot	5/66
Laira	8/67
Newton Abbot	10/71
Withdrawn (Newton Abbot)	2/1/72
(Bristol St Philips Marsh Jct)	8/9/72
(Swindon)	12/9/72
Date cut up	By 13/10/72
Green	24/3/61
OHL flashes	21/10/61
Yellow warning panels	27/12/62
Maroon	-
Blue full yellow ends – double insignia, sans serif, D-prefix	17/9/68
Recorded mileage	1,040,000

D867 ZENITH

D867 ZENITH in green on a freight at Plymouth in May 1966; headboard clip dangling, ventilator flaps open. They often rusted in place like this. ColourRail

ZENITH, now in maroon during the 'double heading period', at Plymouth North Road again, on 24 April 1968. The train is the 08.30 for Paddington and the second Warship is green D866 ZEBRA. J. Binnie.

D867 ZENITH	
To traffic - Laira	26/4/61
Newton Abbot	5/66
Laira	8/67
Withdrawn (Laira)	18/10/71
(Bristol St Philips Marsh Jct)	26/10/71
Component recovery (Laira)	4/7/72
(Bristol St Philips Marsh Jct)	18/8/72
(Swindon)	22/8/72
Date cut up	By 30/9/72
Green	26/4/61
OHL flashes	10/61
Yellow warning panels	1/8/62
Maroon yellow warning panels	By 9/66
Blue full yellow ends – double insignia, sans serif , no D	25/9/70
Recorded mileage	991,000

D868 ZEPHYR

D868 ZEPHYR	
To traffic - Laira	18/5/61
Newton Abbot	5/66
Laira	8/67
Withdrawn (Newton Abbot)	3/10/71
(Bristol St Philips Marsh Jct)	20/10/71
(Swindon)	6/1/72
Date cut up	By 7/4/72
Green	18/5/61
OHL flashes	1/6/62
Yellow warning panels	30/5/63
Maroon	-
Blue full yellow ends – double insignia, serif, D-prefix	By 12/67
Blue full yellow ends – single insignia, serif, no D	6/6/71
Recorded mileage	1,008,000
* repainted at Laira	

D868 ZEPHYR in green at Paignton, 24 July 1966. ColourRail

Blue 868 ZEPHYR, serif number but no D (apparently repainted thus at Laira a few weeks before) at Exeter St David's on 30 July 1971. Train is the 3.30pm Paddington-Paignton.

D869 ZEST

D869 ZEST	
To traffic - Laira	12/7/61
Newton Abbot	5/66
Laira	8/67
Withdrawn (Laira)	30/9/71
(Bristol St Philips Marsh Jct)	By 24/10/71
(Swindon)	16/3/72
Date cut up	By 23/6/72
Green	12/7/61
OHL flashes	By 3/62
Yellow warning panels	21/12/62
Maroon yellow warning panels	By 4/66
Maroon full yellow ends	12/68?
Blue full yellow ends – single insignia, sans serif, no D	9/8/70
Recorded mileage	992,000

All the Zs at Dawlish in May 1969 on the 2.30pm Paddington-Penzance; the view is north-east, station footbridge to the left with the photographer perched above one of the beach access bridges from Station Road. It was curious how the WR, after the first three Pilot Scheme Warships, determined that the names should follow alphabetical order. D869 ZEST heads D870 ZULU, two of the shortest BR locomotive names. Multiple working fittings clear to see.

869 ZEST in blue, Rail Alphabet number and so on, stabled in the yard of the old steam shed at Penzance, 14 June 1961.

D870 ZULU

Maroon D870 ZULU passing Queens Road nearly at Waterloo with the 2.20pm from Exeter, on 3 July 1967. It is late afternoon or early evening at a guess; stock includes BR Mk 1 vehicles in blue and grey with a Bulleid buffet car (probably one of the 'Tavern' rebuilds) as the second coach is still green. The next coach is a Mk.1 dining car - lettered as such on the side. The Brighton line into Victoria passes overhead, towards Battersea Park station and then over Grosvenor Bridge into Victoria to the right. ZULU was the last of the Swindon Warships while a number of the North British ones, though numbered below it, were yet to enter service. It can be readily distinguished from all others from the warning horns on the roof, centrally mounted above the windows. It had been intended to experiment with electric train heating (ETH) and the horns on ZULU were moved up there to free space for the fitting of the ETH gear. As it happened it was not proceeded with but ZULU kept its horns on top. ColourRail

870 ZULU at Gloucester Horton Road on 4 June 1970 with the multiple working equipment in place. In June 1971 ZULU was running light Newton Abbot-Laira when it ran into the rear of a Severn Tunnel Junction-Plymouth Friary freight hauled by 861, near Laira Junction. *ZULU was sent to Swindon for assessment but was eventually withdrawn unrepaired on 28 August. Like 824 HIGHFLYER, it almost got a reprieve when it was sent to Derby RTC in January 1972 to be used in connection with experiments involving gas turbine-hydraulic propulsion. The collision damage meant it was deemed unsuitable and returned to Swindon and cut up in May.* J. Binnie.

D870 ZULU	
To traffic - Laira	25/10/61
Newton Abbot	5/66
Laira	8/67
Stored (Swindon)	18/8/71
Withdrawn (Swindon)	28/8/71
(Derby RTC)	2/1/72
(Swindon)	By 9/1/72
Date cut up	By 12/5/72
Green	25/10/61
OHL flashes	25/10/61
Yellow warning panels	6/5/63
Maroon yellow warning panels	By 12/65
Maroon full yellow ends	5/68
Blue full yellow ends – double insignia, sans serif, no D	By 10/69
Recorded mileage	922,000